Bond Book

This book is part of a special purchas
to upgrade the CALS collection. Fun
the project were approved by Little R
voters on 12/11/07. Thanks, Little Rock!

D0114121

37653015642872
Terry   NonFiction
791.4372 THOMSON
The moment of Psycho : how
Alfred Hitchcock taught
America to love murder

CENTRAL ARKANSAS LIBRARY SYSTEM
ADOLPHINE FLETCHER TERRY
BRANCH LIBRARY
LITTLE ROCK, ARKANSAS

JAN   2010

GAYLORD

THE MOMENT
OF *PSYCHO*

Strangers in the rain.

KODAK PICTURE 1960A

THE MOMENT
OF *PSYCHO*

How ALFRED HITCHCOCK *Taught* AMERICA *to* LOVE MURDER

DAVID THOMSON

BASIC
BOOKS

A Member of the Perseus Books Group
New York

Copyright © 2009 by David Thomson
Published by Basic Books,
A Member of the Perseus Books Group

All rights reserved. Printed in the United States of America. No part
of this book may be reproduced in any manner whatsoever without
written permission except in the case of brief quotations embodied in
critical articles and reviews. For information, address Basic Books,
387 Park Avenue South, New York, NY 10016-8810.

Books published by Basic Books are available at special discounts for
bulk purchases in the United States by corporations, institutions, and
other organizations. For more information, please contact the Special
Markets Department at the Perseus Books Group, 2300 Chestnut
Street, Suite 200, Philadelphia, PA 19103, or call (800) 810-4145,
ext. 5000, or e-mail special.markets@perseusbooks.com.

Designed by Pauline Brown

Library of Congress Cataloging-in-Publication Data

Thomson, David, 1941–
    The moment of Psycho : how Alfred Hitchcock taught America to
love murder / David Thomson.
        p. cm.
    Includes index.
    ISBN 978-0-465-00339-6 (alk. paper)
    1. Psycho (Motion picture : 1960) 2. Hitchcock, Alfred,
1899–1980—Criticism and interpretation. 3. Thrillers (Motion
pictures)—United States—History and criticism. I. Title.

PN1997.P79T46 2009
791.43'72—dc22

                                              2009030821

10 9 8 7 6 5 4 3 2 1

for Greil Marcus

CENTRAL ARKANSAS LIBRARY SYSTEM
ADOLPHINE FLETCHER TERRY BRANCH
LITTLE ROCK, ARKANSAS

CONTENTS

1

1960

THE MOVIES had always encouraged the idea that we were safe, secure, and warm in their dark. It is a comfortable and comforting place to be, for a nickel . . . or $12.50. Come in out of the heat, or the cold. Come in and forget your sorrows and the world's hard times. Our theater has its own air-raid shelter. Take a break at the end of a long day's drive. The cinema is a welcoming motel with fresh linen and a hot shower.

But how far did people trust that promise? The invitation was barbed: yes, we could see women undressing and men shooting guns as if the ammunition was forever. But only because we were not quite there, not in the screen's "there." We were voyeurs, never harmed by the bullets, but never able to handle the women. Yet there is a frisson of danger, too—we feel we can't escape from those dense rows of seated people. What if the building burns from the light of the arc projector? (And films did catch fire in the early days.) What if the "controlled" or censored circumstances of life on-screen suddenly give way to orgy and slaughter? (How dreadful! How delicious!) What if the locomotive comes out of the screen and strikes us? What if the knife we see before our eyes glows and grows until it fits and fills our hand and we are striking, striking? . . .

RIGHT FROM THE START, *Psycho* played with these and darker prospects. The feeling existed that this might be the most excruciatingly skillful film ever made—if you thought of film as a ghost train or a dream, or as an experiment with suspense. Anyone with any sense of film knew not just that *Psycho* changed "cinema" but that now the subversive secret was out—truly this medium was prepared for an outrage in which sex and violence were no longer games but were in fact everything. *Psycho* was so blatant that audiences had to laugh at it, to avoid the giddy swoon of evil and ordeal. The title warned that the central character was a bit of a nut, but the deeper lesson was that the audience in its self-inflicted experiment with danger might be crazy, too. Sex and violence were ready to break out, and censorship crumpled like an old lady's parasol. The orgy had arrived.

* * *

AT THE END OF THE 1950S, Hollywood seemed to be doing its thing in the same old way. It made *The Searchers*, *Rio Bravo*, and *Man of the West*, three of the best Westerns ever done. It produced *Ben-Hur*, *Gigi*, *Giant*, and *Around the World in 80 Days*—large entertainments boundless in budget and scope, but so tame to the imagination. It delivered musicals (*The King and I*, *High Society*, *South Pacific*), Biblical epics (*The Ten Commandments*), and inspiring stories of humanity and sacrifice (*The Diary of Anne Frank*, *The Defiant Ones*). And all these films ended well. Most had happy endings; even where Anne Frank died we were assured that her enemies were eventually defeated and that Anne's virtue was an endless flame. Off to one side, there were a few unaccountable personal visions, movies about some inner America, full of dread and disorder—*Kiss Me Deadly*, *Bigger Than Life*, *The Night of the Hunter*, *Sweet Smell of Success*, *Some Like It Hot*—glimpses of a real but alarming society (most of them still in black-and-white because it was "harsh"). But these were not the films Hollywood regarded as important.

The people who had founded the business were dying off. Those left told themselves movies were better than ever, and they said they were still in charge. But they were old men who did not realize how fast public taste was changing. There were already shrewd observers who saw that the big thing—the golden age, the unquestioning marriage of Hollywood and America—was over. Sometimes it seemed that the ugly aftermath of goldenness, *The Tarnished Angels* (and that was a current title, too), was what the new fragmented films were revealing.

In 1958 American box office dropped below $1 billion a year, a figure it had held since the early 1940s. In the same year, the average weekly attendance at the movies fell to 35 million; it had been 82 million in 1946. Another statistic helped explain that decline. In the '50s, the number of American households with television went up from about 4 million to about 48 million. There wasn't any question about America's, or the world's, delight in moving picture stories. But staying at home with them felt easier, cheaper, and more natural. No matter how big or spectacular Hollywood made the movies, the audience took the smaller version. One of the most brilliant people in the city saw that light, and in the mid-1950s he augmented his theatrical pictures with a new TV series. It changed him more than he could have guessed.

When Alfred Hitchcock turned sixty on August 13, 1959, he was already the best-known film director in the United States. People liked his films: in the fifties *Strangers on a Train*, *Dial M for Murder*, *Rear Window*, *To Catch a Thief*, *The Man Who Knew Too Much*, and *North by Northwest* had all been popular hits, suspense stories served with the black cream of Hitchcock's humor. There had been other films—*I Confess*, *The Wrong Man*, *The Trouble with Harry*, and *Vertigo*—that had not been as successful. Still, Hitchcock's output in the fifties had been extraordinary, and in France, for example, he was widely regarded as a great artist. Two critics on their way to becoming filmmakers, Claude Chabrol and Eric Rohmer, had written a book about Hitchcock in 1957. A book about a filmmaker! It was a great novelty. In the fifties film was still so central as an entertainment that no one thought to write books about it.

Hitchcock had earned an uncommon reputation not just for suspense and mystery but for artful, teasing games played with moral responsibility. There were ways in which he asserted or advertised himself. He had a habit of putting himself in his own films—for a shot or a cameo moment—and the habit had become famous if only because the round, respectable, and sedate-looking Hitchcock was at odds with the frantic action in his films. (You could hardly imagine Hitch in *North by Northwest* racing Cary Grant into the cornfield as the crop-dusting aircraft turned ugly. Nor could you picture Hitch himself drawing all those gorgeous women into embraces that seemed to go a few inches further—and inches count—than censorship wished for.)

But it was in the '50s that this public recognition of Hitchcock was deepened by his new TV show, *Alfred Hitchcock Presents*. The show started playing in the fall of 1955 and would run for ten years. It was a showcase for mystery stories, often very well written and directed. Hitchcock even directed a few of the shows himself. But he graced every edition with a short on-camera introduction and farewell. These highlight spots stressed his fastidious, plummy way of speaking and his rather chilly, formal humor. They offered an intriguing contrast between nasty material and classy presentation, and they established Hitch (coming and going to lugubrious music, Gounod's "Funeral March of a Marionette") as a droll fellow who liked to make audiences sweat. The marketing of *Psycho* would draw upon this famous framework in a striking way—one that emphasized the fact of a Hitchcock film. These TV shows were filmed at the premises of Revue, the production company that had been set up by Hitchcock's preeminent agent, Lew Wasserman.

HITCHCOCK TOOK FILM—as a craft, an art, or a way of controlling information—very seriously. Nothing else mattered as much to him. He wanted to produce a great surge of emotion in his public—but he was very vague as to what emotion. So it became fear, or terror. And terror, sooner or later, wants power. He was generally very modest about his own artistic efforts, because he knew such talk was frowned upon in the film industry. As a younger man, beginning in the twenties, he had sometimes been accused of artiness. But in the fifties he was flattered by the way young French writers took him so seriously, for at a repressed level he had very large creative ambitions. So in films like *Strangers on a Train*, *Rear Window*, and *Vertigo*, he had been pursuing the issue of moral responsibility in voyeurism and the larger question of why "decent" people were so interested in visions of crime and violence and sex that they could watch in apparent safety or immunity.

At the end of *Rear Window*, when James Stewart, by dint of constant spying, has worked out that a man in the courtyard he surveys has killed his wife, that man comes to Stewart's apartment. We expect menace and danger. Instead, the man asks, "What do you want of me?" And Hitchcock clearly was fascinated by what it was the "good" characters in films, and their audience, wanted. It is still an abiding question, the one that asks not just what are the movies for? But what are we for?

Moreover, it's clear in hindsight that Hitchcock was personally caught up in that voyeurism and its consequences. He had been fat as long as anyone remembered. He was married to a valued assistant, Alma. They had a daughter, Patricia. His life seemed settled. But, secretly, Hitch was in the habit of falling in love with his actresses and making the film speak to that infatuation—with Joan Fontaine, with Ingrid Bergman, with Grace Kelly, with Kim Novak, with Eva Marie Saint. This is not just gossip or speculation. Throughout the fifties (his best work) the films are charged with the lust and guilt of watching a beloved figure under stress. In *Psycho* another such woman—Janet Leigh—is remorselessly studied for forty minutes and then torn to pieces.

Hitch was a success. He had had a bad patch at the box office in the late '40s (*Rope, Under Capricorn, Stage Fright*), but most of his films did well. He lived in Beverly Hills in tasteful luxury (with a weekend retreat in Santa Cruz), yet he had been the son of an East London greengrocer, a lowly figure in the British class system. But Hitchcock had never—and would never—win an Oscar as Director. His first film in America, *Rebecca*, had won Best Picture, but that award went to its producer, David O. Selznick—and Hitch had a poor opinion of Selznick. Hitch had been nominated for directing *Rebecca*, as he would be for *Lifeboat, Spellbound*, and *Rear Window*. Actors might win working for him (Fontaine in *Suspicion*), but even that was a rarity. And Hitch was not even nominated for *Notorious, Strangers on a Train, Vertigo*, or *North by Northwest*. Why was that so? The simple answer is that his pursuit of suspenseful violence was deemed so tongue-in-cheek as to lack gravity or seriousness. The Academy has seldom been long on humor, and some felt Hitch did not respect subject matter enough. This attitude affected more than the Oscars. Hitchcock was never honored by the Directors Guild or the BAFTAs (the British awards) and only once by the New York Film Critics—for

The Lady Vanishes in 1938. In time these omissions were regretted: the Academy gave Hitchcock its Thalberg Award in 1967, and the American Film Institute made him its Life Achievement honoree in 1979. But the Academy never exercised the gesture that it has made for so many (Chaplin, Griffith, Welles, Renoir, Lubitsch, Hawks, Keaton): the awarding of an honorary Oscar for career achievement so as to make up for missed opportunities over the years.

It's not so remarkable to conclude that Hitch was hurt or offended, as to wonder why the oversight occurred. No one doubted his ability, technically, as an entertainer or as a master of suspense. But the public and the Academy alike failed to esteem his humor or to see it as part of an earnest approach. It may have had something to do with his perceived smugness and the way an Englishman had dodged the war and learned the ways of the studio system better than most Americans.

That mixture of the threatening and the sardonic (a tone to be found in Harold Pinter, another East London artist from lowly origins) would be put to the test in the years around 1960. And the test fixed on the different appreciation of Hitch in France and English-speaking countries. A key experience for Hitch was going to the French Riviera to shoot *To Catch a Thief* in 1954, for it was during that work that he was first approached by young French critics—like François Truffaut, Jacques Rivette, and Jean-Luc Godard. They interviewed him for *Cahiers du Cinema* and devoted an entire issue of the magazine to him, that of October 1954. They told him how great he was. And then, in the late '50s, they seemed to vindicate that praise by themselves becoming notable filmmakers. It was at the Cannes Film Festival of May 1959 (just months before *Psycho* was settled on as a project) that François Truffaut—Hitch's great champion in France—won the director's prize for his first film, *Les 400 Coups*.

French admiration didn't mean too much in Hollywood eyes—or not yet. *Cahiers du Cinema* had modest sales. The films by Truffaut and Godard would play in art houses. But it was in the '60s that French ideas on cinema were taken up in America as the study of film gripped American higher education. In the space of ten years, a subject taught, gingerly, in a handful of places became a mainstream college major. In other words, films were no longer just the property of the business that made them.

And it was the same younger generation, equipped with the Pill and a new attitude toward sex, that began to chafe at movie censorship. *Psycho* was ahead of those changes, but it was ahead of everything: we should never forget that it indulged sex (nakedness) and violence (that knife) and told censorship to get lost. Many people condemned that audacity; some thought it was trashy. But Hitchcock carried discretion past all known codes and guessed that the audience was ready. *Psycho* played in first-rank theaters, it made a fortune, and quite quickly it would be talked of as brilliant "art" by a young generation that wanted to acclaim film and its modernity. No one had nursed the idea that film could be art more carefully than Alfred Hitchcock.

So the sixty-year-old had things to prove and matters of superiority to demonstrate. I do not mean to say he was consumed by bitterness, though he was wounded by the halfhearted response to *Vertigo*. Hitch understood his own work—there is even a case to be made that it was too thoroughly premeditated—and he grasped the tortured reflection of directors and actresses he had delivered in *Vertigo*. It was not far from a confession, though one that very few had seemed to understand. Its greatness had been missed, and its narrative suspense failed at the box office. Hitch may have reckoned that Kim Novak had proved an inadequate substitute for Vera Miles (his first choice for the lead) or the regal Grace Kelly.

Like so many in the audience, Hitch adored Kelly—in *Dial M for Murder*, *Rear Window*, and *To Catch a Thief*, her puree of comedy, class, and sex suited him perfectly, and it was delivered with a cool, glassy style that he cherished. It wasn't his fault that she'd found a prince in the South of France, and clearly he lived with the dream of reclaiming her. But that was coupled with a raw, antagonistic urge—to be naughty, to challenge Hollywood on nearly every standard he could find. And, make no mistake, *Psycho* was a piece of insurrectionary defiance.

In late 1958, to follow *North by Northwest*, Hitchcock was contemplating an English novel, *No Bail for the Judge*, by Henry Cecil. It turned on a judge's daughter, to be played by Audrey Hepburn, who sets out to prove her father's innocence in a murder case. Next to *Psycho*, it seems nearly archaic, but there was an attempted rape scene in the treatment that made Hepburn flinch. So that project lapsed, and in June 1959 Hitchcock began to talk about *Psycho*.

Robert Bloch's novel of the same name had been around in proof for a few months. It was based on the activity of a serial killer from Wisconsin, Ed Gein, who had been captured in 1957. Like Gein, Bloch was from Wisconsin, increasingly fascinated by what he learned of the murders.

Bloch was a writer of horror fiction, but now he was drawn to the real-crime aspects of the Gein story. "In my mind," he would say later, "the character would have been the equivalent of a Rod Steiger type at that time, who lived alone—a recluse more or less, who didn't have a lot of friends. How would he select his victims? I came up with his being a motel-keeper because of easy access to strangers." Bloch also dreamed up the killing in a shower stall. He reckoned that was the epitome of invaded privacy. But his novel had the killer's knife, in one stroke, slashing through the shower curtain and beheading the woman. For Hitchcock, that killing was all too rapid. From the outset, he saw the shower murder as a set piece, an extended frenzy of blows that might take a week to film.

But studios had passed because of the unwholesome subject matter: a fellow who runs a rural motel, a guy fat and forty who is a serial killer and keeps the stuffed body of his mother. This was creepy "shocker" material—pulp fiction, if you like—though it's worth recalling that Truman Capote's *In Cold Blood* would be a literary rescue of similar material. And the dates are suggestive: the *New York Times* story from Holcomb, Kansas, about the slaughter of four Clutter family members, appeared in November 1959.

I doubt there's any way of establishing whether the number of wanton killing sprees in rural America picked up in the 1950s (though a case can be made that the spread of local television news brought extra attention to such lurid local discoveries). It may just be that such murders began to be more widely reported and that they struck "tender" urban sensibilities like those of Hitchcock and Capote as revealing of the allegedly placid hinterland. Capote surprised his friends by finding the crime fascinating and exemplary. Hitchcock was struck by the Gein story and with what Bloch had made of it. Not that Hitch was a devotee of rural life. Most of his films are urban stories with sophisticated characters who seldom stray too far from cocktails and the club. I don't see anyone in his work foreshadowing Norman Bates. Which is not to say that Hitch hadn't been struck by the way a new kind of character might loom up out of nowhere. How had Elvis Presley or James Dean become American phenomena? And how could any observer miss the emotional anger or the brooding violence in those country boys?

In film, or television, in the 1950s, domestic horror was in short supply. There are only two pictures I can think of that come anywhere near it, one of which is Charles Laughton's *The Night of the Hunter*, in which a rural "preacher" (Robert Mitchum) hunts down two children in a dark fairy-tale landscape from nightmare. But Laughton's film was a disaster, in great part because there was so little tradition of American Gothic or ugly violence and so little attention to abnormal behavior.

The other film was Orson Welles's *Touch of Evil*, shot in the rancid remains of Venice, California, and quite simply certain that small-town America was run by monsters. Of course, Welles did something else prescient in that film: he chose Janet Leigh as the icon of a decent America opposed to this filth. To the best of my knowledge, Hitchcock never owned up to having seen *Touch of Evil*, but the influence is palpable (both films employed Robert Clatworthy as assistant set designer). And the "night man" at the motel in the Welles film—a daring portrait by Dennis Weaver—is a piece of work that one can imagine Anthony Perkins studying with delight as he developed Norman Bates.

The only other functioning crazy in American film then was Jerry Lewis—which is not a flippant observation. Lewis was getting at the underside of America, as Dean and Presley were attempting. But no one would have dared think of Presley in *Psycho* (until you have the idea, and then you can't get rid of it).

There was just one area where trash was thriving in American film—in the B pictures being made by Roger Corman. Above all, Corman had seen that rock and roll signaled a teenage audience, ready for a new level of violence, splashy, gaudy, and lip smacking. Corman worked in other genres—music pictures, Edgar Allan Poe, and gangster remakes—but a few of his pictures were mining the ground for *Psycho: A Bucket of Blood* (notice the insolence of the title) and *The Little Shop of Horrors* (which was early Jack Nicholson, another intriguing Norman).

PARAMOUNT SAID they were frightened of *Psycho*. The killing was brutal yet ordinary. The setting was commonplace. The script called for a bathroom and a lavatory, as well as an extended slaughter! The studio aligned itself with middle-aged decorum in reckoning that *Psycho* was going too far.

The talent agency MCA had purchased Universal in November 1958—and it was through MCA that Lew Wasserman served as Hitch's agent. MCA bought the rights to the Bloch novel for $9,000, but in so discreet a way that Bloch did not realize that Hitch was after him. James Cavanagh was hired to do a screenplay (he had done several episodes of the Hitchcock TV show). And

Paramount started pressing Hitch on whether the project was advisable.

This is when Wasserman made one of his master strokes. He proposed that *Psycho* would be a Hitchcock picture on which Paramount had only 40 percent of the ownership. Hitch would defer his salary and direct the film free of charge on a budget kept as low as possible. Indeed, Hitch offered to do it like one of his TV shows—cut-price, very fast, without the production values of the Paramount films, without color or big stars. In return, Hitch would own 60 percent of the picture himself. Wasserman even came up with this topper: to save Paramount from embarrassment, the picture would be shot over at Universal on cheaply rented sets.

This astonishing deal only occurred because top executives at Paramount—like Frank Freeman and Barney Balaban (men in their seventies, unaware how far America and the world would vote for sex and violence in the sixties)—were so put off by *Psycho* and its threat of violence. But the consequence of the deal was remarkable. For the first time in his career, Hitch was in a position to make a fortune as a major profit participant. The man who had served Paramount so well never made another picture there.

As good as his word, Hitchcock hired John L. Russell as cameraman on *Psycho* (Russell was a veteran from *Alfred Hitchcock Presents* and camera operator on *Touch of Evil*), and he agreed not to exceed a budget of $800,000. The decor would be especially mean, with down-market interiors throughout. The cast was small. The driving scenes were all back projection. Two or three reels were virtually silent! It was back to basics, as well as a bomb beneath the city.

Cavanagh proved a flop as a writer, and he was replaced by Joseph Stefano. Stefano stayed as faithful as possible to the Bloch novel—but he was writing for Anthony Perkins, who, far from fat and forty, had a real youth following by then. Perkins owed Paramount a picture, and he signed on for $40,000. Janet Leigh came later, for $25,000, after Hitchcock had considered Eva Marie Saint, Hope Lange, and even Lana Turner. If there was a crucial edge in the casting, it was that both Perkins and Leigh were appealing, and like people from next door. And it was Stefano who found the structure in which part 1 would be Marion's story and part 2 Norman's. By the third week of November they were shooting.

By Christmas, Marion Crane was in the swamp.

2

Continuity

HOTEL

THANK GOD IT'S FRIDAY, except that in this part of America, in Phoenix, Arizona, God seems a long way away. But Phoenix grows out of the desert, and the Bible is a book with many desert scenes.

You can make 1960 sound comfortable, corny, and fifty years ago. Dwight Eisenhower was president still, but he was about to be retired because of two full terms, mounting illness, and the gap between his paternal bearing and the opportunistic times. Richard Nixon and John Kennedy lived in that difference. They were both trickier men than Eisenhower understood, far more prepared to do whatever they had to do to win. In 1960 they ran a very close race in which the fighting was nasty, dirty, and as expected. It was

American, and in the first forty minutes of *Psycho*—the unease before its storm—it is remarkable how many glimpses Alfred Hitchcock allows of a grasping, devious, and ordinarily nasty nation.

Now, being nasty is not the same as cutting an unknown woman to pieces, and *Psycho*'s significance is in going so much further than filmgoers anticipated. But the nastiness can be felt like sandpaper. Fifty years later, this abrasiveness or indifference is a better explanation of the film's central violence than the cockamamie answer it concocts about a boy being possessed now and then by the angry spirit of his dead mother. The central killing grows out of the grim unkindness of the world we have seen, not from the lurid casebook of the Bates family.

So we begin in Phoenix, Arizona, at 2:43 on the afternoon of Friday, December 11. But while the title-sequence verticals by Saul Bass are pure and bold, Phoenix seems drab in its winter light. The photography has no direct sunlight, so the grays of concrete and stone recede into the same hues in the desert mountains. Nor are we shown a famous Sun Belt city, or the touristy views of fair Phoenix. Instead, we close in on one furtive window in an ugly building, open a crack with the blinds down nearly all the way. The room seems gloomy, uninviting. But the camera slips in nonetheless, as if to say that spying is normal.

Psycho would be a very different film if we came in on Sam Loomis and Marion Crane (John Gavin and Janet Leigh) naked, making love, in rapture. And, more or less, we are led to suppose that that's what we would have seen if we'd come earlier—at 2:13, say. But the time is precise, and it makes our visit seem appointed. So it's important to note that we see the aftermath of sex: a woman, a blonde, back in her underwear, stretched out on the bed, and a man naked above the waist standing beside her. There's something in the air that makes sex itself seem illicit.

The two are lovers, but their love has come and gone, without our seeing it. And without them being transformed by it. Their hair is combed, and the sweat has been wiped away. So now they are partners in a transaction, beginning to go their separate ways. If there was no talk, you might conclude from their actions and appearance that she is a hooker and he is a client. She wears a bra and a slip— and in the code of 1960 that is "naked," just as it was unprecedented in an opening "information" scene like this. But in fact it is an erotic restriction, no less professional when Marion Crane gets up and dresses fully. It is a bare room—the kind they can rent by the hour—and the light is harsh. Nothing is kind to their love or their assignation. If sex was intended as an escape (that is often its role in American film), the texture of this film offers no support to the hope.

They are acting like a man and a whore, or like lovers who must not be seen. And the talk (if we turn that on, too) is a steady conflict between romance and money. They are lovers. But he was married to someone else and is trapped now by the grip of alimony and his father's debts. They are not as young as springtime: Janet Leigh in 1960 was thirty-three and John Gavin thirty-two. Marion says she has never been married, but she has a ripe carnal body and a face that seems to know about sex—even if it was sex with Tony Curtis.

And here we need to stress one quite remarkable thing: an American film has begun (in the famously developing city of Phoenix—a miracle of new urban life) in which the hopes and desires of two mature people are overshadowed by lack of money and social freedom. Look at a hundred other films from the '50s and you will not find the same cramped air. As a rule, the rooms are larger and brighter than they would be in reality, waiting to be filled by the hopes and energies of the era. Most films of the '50s are secret ads for the American way of life. *Psycho* is a warning about its lies and limits.

Nor is it clear how these two are going to escape: the alimony is a dead weight on their prospects. When they part, they do not have a date or a hope for the future. So there will be more lunchtime hotel rooms, apparently. The last image of the scene is Sam alone in the room, standing up but bowed down, more a victim than a hero. Marion hurries back to her office, and Sam goes to the airport to get a plane to Fairvale, California, where he has a hardware store and lives in the storeroom behind it.

So they live apart. Of course, they have occasional sex, but we did not see it. We simply watched the assembled parts for sex and asked ourselves what Marion might look like without these comprehensive bras she's wearing (I'd guess a good 36 D-cup). But guessing is a fool's romance.

OFFICE

When Marion gets back to the office, she has a headache instead of the calm that might have followed sex. There's a lovely dissolve from the hotel room to the office (looking out on the street) so that the dejected figure of Sam in the room rhymes with another figure on the sidewalk—a stout man made funnier by his cowboy hat, his back to the camera. It is Alfred Hitchcock, letting us know how indifferent he is to Sam's mood and not noticing Marion hurrying around behind him to enter the office. Such cameos are supposedly playful. But this dissolve carries a sinister edge.

Marion has a friend in the office—she is Caroline, played by Patricia Hitchcock, the director's daughter. Hitch never gave his daughter a break in his films. So she is smug, gossipy, nasty, and vain here. She may be Marion's friend, but you know she'd say anything behind her back.

Caroline reassures Marion: the boss of the realty company is still at his business lunch. She gloats over the way her husband, Teddy, called her, and her mother (to see if Teddy called). Caroline is self-satisfied, antilife, and uncharitable, all in a few lines and twenty seconds. You never forget her naggy voice or the aggrieved tone in all the supporting parts that fill the first part of the film.

Take the boss, Mr. Lowery, who soon arrives with his client, Cassidy. The boss is a rat and the client a bullfrog. They have done their deal, and Cassidy is drunk, sexually overconfident, and dead set on Marion. He sits on her desk. He describes how his eighteen-year-old daughter is getting married, leaving him free—for Marion. And he talks about using money to buy off unhappiness. He waves a wad of bills—not battered singles but slick new hundreds—under her nose. "I never carry more than I can afford to lose," he says, and Marion knows exactly what he means. (She really could have been a hooker once.)

"He was flirting with you," says Caroline, as the two men go into an inner office for another drink. "I guess he must have noticed my wedding ring."

Yet flirting carries hints of romance or fondness. Cassidy was propositioning Marion. He was seeing whether he could buy her. And he may have been a little more pushy because he sensed her amused resistance. So he does not notice that his money may have invaded her imagination.

Marion takes some papers that need signing into the inner office. She asks if she can go home early because of her headache. Lowery consents, but Cassidy suggests a weekend in Las Vegas instead. "I'm going to spend this weekend in bed, thank you," says Marion. But she agrees to take the $40,000 in cash and deposit it at the bank on her way home. (She still needs to be laid.)

ANOTHER ROOM

As a top secretary in Phoenix, Arizona, in 1960, let's say that Marion Crane earned $100 a week. In her "home," in Phoenix, we see her standing in the doorway to a closet, wearing a black slip and a black bra, and looking wistfully at the envelope of money, which is the only thing on her bed. A close-up peeps into the envelope, and we can read the top bill in the piles of hundreds.

The only felt sound is that of Bernard Herrmann's music, plucked strings or water dripping, inner music, that of thought coming slowly toward a dire decision. The room is just that, a single room not much better than the hotel we saw earlier. Marion cannot really afford an apartment, and she has not done much to make this room personal or her own. It feels like another nondescript room for rent. And there is Marion, in her underwear for the second time already—alone with the money, the music, and the camera. Of course, she does not argue the matter out with herself—shall I? shan't I?—but we know she is sliding toward the wrong decision. For she has a suitcase that she is packing already. As well as the black bra. It is a scene that Janet Leigh plays with absolute authority—and I would still employ it as an audition for promising actresses, and as a test of physical presence.

Nothing is said. Her decision is folly, but the impulse is irresistible. The decision is plainly human, but the aura of fantasy or speculation—the overall, "Would you? . . ."—is beautifully embodied in the stealthy, private action we behold and gradually become complicit in. It is because we have to work out what she is thinking that we recognize the alluring prospect of taking the $40,000. And the observation of the decision is eroticized by the music, by the feeling of this hapless woman alone in her room, and by the film's steady nagging away at her nakedness.

She decides—yet she can tell herself that she will really make the decision later. For the moment, she can say, she has slipped the envelope and its money into her handbag so that it will be safe. Then she picks up the case and is on her way. The shot of her leaving the room dissolves to the first head-on close-up of her driving for her life and her soul.

THE ROAD

So what kind of film is *Psycho* so far? A theft has occurred, though you could argue that Marion has not entirely let the thief into the open. But that is settled for her in a clinching touch of small embarrassment. As she is driving out of Phoenix, she stops at a pedestrian crossing, and Lowery and Cassidy step out to cross the road in front of her. Only Lowery sees her, and he smiles—because it is Marion—but then he does a slight double take because she had told him she was going to bed. This looks like a lie, and for a moment that is worse than theft. It is not the end of the world, but it is as incriminating as Lowery's anxious gaze, straight into the camera. She will be a thief next. And so this Arizona version of Emma Bovary has let her life slip closer to fate and fatality. We like her. A part of us wants her. But we behold her making her way and her mistakes. We are sympathetic, but we are scolding her, too, and Herrmann's music raises its accusatory tone.

That Friday afternoon, setting off at about four o'clock, Marion will drive to the outskirts of Gorman, in California. This is some 350 miles, going on Interstate 10 or 40, with a great stretch of Mojave Desert to cross, before she is in the foothills north of Los Angeles. But if she goes to Gorman, then she is headed for I-5, the highway that runs north and south in California. We gather that she is heading for "Fairvale," where Sam lives. There is not a Fairvale to be found in that state, though it has Fair Oaks, Fair Play, Fairfield, Farehaven, Fairmead, and Fairview. A place has been invented, perhaps to avoid any later thought that the Bates family lived in this or that town. But Marion drives a long way that first night and then a little farther on the Saturday before night and rain stop her, and that means that Fairvale is most likely in the area of Redding or Shasta—northern California, deep country, not too heavily populated, then or now.

Of course, *Psycho* is a period film, even if it makes such use of the freeway system brought to fruition by President Eisenhower in the 1950s. How is it period? Marion never phones Sam to say she is coming. She has no cell phone. She never stops to call and seek his advice. That tells us something about their separated love life: the telephone is likely too expensive as a way of keeping in touch.

Which makes it that much more poignant, or desperate, that Marion is driving more than 800 miles to be with her man and to deposit her crime in his lap or bank. And she drives, making light of the great journey and the dissolves that carry her on into desert, night, and the great distances of the West.

Then it is morning. We see Marion's car pulled off the highway, by the roadside. Another car—a highway patrol car—appears in the same picture. It stops, and an officer gets out to investigate. This policeman is not nasty, like the other small roles she meets. But he is a looming figure of authority and question, the embodiment of her paranoia. He is not named, but he is played by Mort Mills (an actor who had just had a key supporting role in Orson Welles's *Touch of Evil*). Hitchcock treats him as a uniform, a peaked cap, a chiseled face, and dark glasses that are never removed—he's like a comic-book cop. And he looks straight into the camera, into her car, and into Marion Crane. She is asleep, but his intrusion wakes her and fills her with dread.

She tells him she pulled off the road the night before because she was afraid of falling asleep. He says there are plenty of motels around "just to be safe." "Have I broken any law?" she asks, getting tougher with the impersonal face. "No, ma'am," he says. In truth, he is considerate and gentle with her. But she is behaving oddly, so he asks to see her license. She's free to go, but as she drives off she sees in her rearview mirror that he's following her. This is a lovely moment in which the strands of highway seem to make a knot behind her.

At a junction, with roads to Bakersfield or Los Angeles, she slips into Gorman. She has made another foolish decision. The cop has her license plate number, so she reckons to exchange her car for another. Marion is hardly her own best friend (in this first section of the film, "psycho" could only apply to her). Having committed a foolish crime (though one that might still be repaired if she drove back to Phoenix), she now compounds it.

CALIFORNIA CHARLIE

He is a car salesman on the edge of the desert—tall, thin, dried out, full of zigzag hype, in a polka-dotted bow tie but absolutely certain that the desert will outlast every vehicle he sells. It is a one-scene performance, given to John Anderson, a polished, contained actor. And he is so exact, so studied and dark, that he reduces Marion Crane to wreckage. She drives away from his premises, her fear and energy multiplied; the exchange with Charlie is like a rehearsal for being cut to pieces. She has been undermined, chopped off at the ankles.

Because one cop has seen her driving with Arizona plates, she reckons to trade in her car for a California model. It is a demented action, aggravated by the way the highway patrolman pulls in to observe the transaction—an extra that Charlie cannot miss. He's ready to hustle her into a deal, only to discover that her panic to swap cars is breathless and lethal. It is as if she has an inner dream of never going back to Arizona again, or of running without any discretion or pretense.

She looks at another car—any other car—and decides that's the one. She rejects any need for a test drive. And when Charlie proposes, "I'd figure your car plus . . . $700," she repeats the sum (clearly outrageous). "Ah," he butts in, "you always got time to argue money, huh?" She slams the door shut and accepts the terms. He wonders then if she has the title—can she prove it's her car?

She goes into the ladies' room with her handbag and a copy of the *Los Angeles Times* she bought at a stand. She can't see anything about her theft. But in the cramped cubicle, jammed up against a mirror and her reflection, she takes out the money and peels off seven $100 bills. Benjamin Franklins.

Charlie still wants her to test the car—a white Ford. The cop is across the road watching. Charlie has a smarting conscience about the rough deal he's laid on this pretty woman. But Marion won't wait. Indeed, she very nearly drives the new car off the lot without having her suitcase carried over from the old car. The last shot of this magnificent trap of a sequence is that of the three men in a line—Charlie, the cop, and the guy who brought the suitcase—watching her dust and her demonic need to get away. She has made her madness clear, but three in a row—male, without understanding, but upright in suspicion—they are like her Furies. Will she ever find peace, or is she about to drive off into the northwest, driving for 40,000 miles?

NIGHTMARE

The tension is building. Marion has gone a little crazy: her behavior with the cars was flagrant and irrational, whereas the passage where she actually "stole" the money was a lulling fantasy. But crazy Marion becomes much more of a person.

She drives on, northward, with that same head-on close-up that Hitchcock used yesterday, back in Phoenix. It lets us study Marion without her knowing it: it is a grilling and an interrogation from a concealed vantage. And now she cracks. Her voiceover begins to fill the picture with imagined talk—talk about her, talk the Furies might exchange. And as this tirade against her goes on, so night falls.

We hear the car dealer and the highway patrolman talking behind her back. Then the radio melodrama switches to Phoenix where Lowery and Caroline are on the phone together working it out that Marion has run away and the money is missing. Lowery goes to Cassidy, and we see the anguished face of Marion smile with dark sexual knowingness as Cassidy growls, "Well, I ain't about to kiss off $40,000! I'll get it back, and if any of it's missin' I'll replace it with her fine soft flesh! I'll track her, never you doubt it!"

Her smile acknowledges the cruelty implicit in voyeurism—and, of course, it's not just Cassidy who has been giving her the searching eye. It's us, the audience, studying her as a kind of sexual offering or bait.

Then the night turns to rain: and now there is an odd feeling of Marion being trapped by the aridity of the car—a long drive is physically exhausting, yet the "pool" beats against the car without healing or refreshing her. Put another way, she is "in" a shower, yet cut off from it.

All the while, on this drive, Bernard Herrmann's music has been building in stress and pain, turning the screws on folly and ordeal—no matter that for now Marion is most threatened by the voices she imagines.

Oncoming headlights dazzle her. In the wash of light on her windshield and through the harsh movement of her wipers, she sees a sign, Bates Motel—Vacancy. Didn't the patrolman urge her to think of motels, and their safety? Doesn't she deserve a little rest?

It's only later that one realizes how in this night drive, in mounting distress, she can conjure up the voices of her "enemies"—Charlie, the cop, Caroline, Lowery, and Cassidy. But she never brings Sam's voice in. You can argue that she leaves him out because she knows he will berate her for behaving so foolishly. But there's another, sadder, thought—that Marion's hard life is that much worse because she may not really love Sam after all. I put it that way because she is now about to meet someone who looks a lot like Sam and is by far the most sensitive and kind person the picture has had to offer.

BROTHERS

At night, in the rain, we realize something about the motel that was not apparent from the road. It is two antagonistic forms. At the road, the motel is a series of bungalow cabins—long, horizontal, like cars themselves. But on higher ground above these buildings there stands a large Gothic house, almost certainly with a cellar and attics as well as two full stories. This house was located in some form on the Universal lot, and it was then improved and decorated and put up near the low-slung cabins. As such, it resembles the house painted by Edward Hopper in *House by the Railroad*, from 1925—that house is larger but on very much the same plan, and in Hopper's painting it stands out against a pale stretched sky like a skull. There's a striking contrast in the juxtaposition of the old vertical "home" and the horizontal abode for transients. It grows odder the more you think about it, for these two buildings are less brothers than parent and child. But if you have the large house standing there, why not use it as a hotel? Most of the lights in the rooms of the house are on—they seem to be burning. The light is so intense it has flared away the outline of the windows.

Then a man comes out of the house and down the steps that lead to the motel. He is tall and dark, and he looks like Sam Loomis, but freer, more relaxed: Anthony Perkins was twenty-seven, only a few years younger than John Gavin, and coltlike. "Dirty night," he says to Marion. He is Norman Bates, and he lets her into the office. She asks if there is a vacancy. "Twelve cabins—twelve vacancies," he admits. He has his own sad humor.

It seems that the motel has gone "dead" after they moved the highway away. It's the story of a good country road being usurped by the new highways of the '50s. "We just keep on lighting the lights and following the formalities," says Norman. There's self-pity there, yet he seems uncomplaining. Norman often talks in two voices. Marion signs the motel register as "Marie Samuels" (she does think of Sam) from Los Angeles. Norman puts her in cabin 1, next to the office. It's only then that she wonders about food. There's a big diner up the road, he tells her, "just outside of Fairvale." Fairvale, her destination, is only fifteen miles away. And in America, fifteen miles is a moment.

But she doesn't decide to drive on. Norman shows her to her cabin. The rather shy boy is hesitant about mentioning "the bathroom." He admits it's stuffy in her cabin and opens a window. There are pictures of birds on the walls, but the room is nondescript—like the others in the film so far—even if the bathroom burns very brightly (it must have about twice the power of illumination it would have in reality).

Norman is Anthony Perkins, and we can feel the idea that Perkins and Leigh were the only two players in the film whom Hitchcock liked or was interested in. Though Norman is shy, the scene slips along on small talk and we suddenly feel the different temperature: here are two characters who want to like each other. He tells her his name, and he guesses that the diner feels too far away for her. So he invites her to share his supper—a sandwich and a glass of milk—up at the big house. "I'd like to," says Marion. She is not stirred by this man, or attracted, except by his civility, his decency, and his longing to be friendly.

Hitchcock had met Perkins in the summer of 1959, before there was a script for the picture. He had liked him immediately. The actor had been in *The Actress*, *Friendly Persuasion*, and *Fear Strikes Out*. He had tried to be the young man opposite Sophia Loren in *Desire Under the Elms*. The audience did not know that Perkins was gay, but it was understood in Hollywood. He was also smart, hip, funny, well read—the kind of actor Hitch enjoyed. No one else was considered for the part, and the scriptwriter,

Joseph Stefano, was told to write for Perkins—young, eager, nervous, insecure, maybe a touch feminine.

It was later on that Hitchcock thought of casting Stuart Whitman as Sam Loomis. Whitman was thirty-three, notably rugged or masculine. He could have played Sam, but Hitchcock then yielded to the suggestion of agent Lew Wasserman and cast John Gavin. He thought Gavin was less interesting as an actor, but that hardly mattered since he was not interested in Sam. Still, later on, there are scenes between Sam and Norman where Hitch seems struck by their resemblance and frames a scene so as to stress it.

This affinity is one of those things latent in the film without being developed. But that doesn't make it unimportant. For we the viewers see it and feel it, and it alters our sense of the triangle. Sam may be her lover, but Norman actually talks to Marion—on a first meeting—with more sympathy than Sam seems to possess. Norman is the more sensitive of the two. She may guess he is gay (or shy), but that doesn't mean that her mind is unaffected by the meeting. Marion Crane is on a strange pilgrimage, and we are about to lose her. But Norman is the character who allows for her redemption. It's because of that, I think, that losing her becomes so hard. A subtler point, not really explored, is whether the most emotionally discerning people in life are those who live closest to disturbance.

"NOT HERSELF"

Alone in cabin 1, Marion starts to unpack her suitcase. We get a better look at the motel room: it is actually a rather richer room than her place in Phoenix. There are inner net curtains and outer heavy drapes. The light in the room reaches up to the ceiling so that it feels comfortable and secure. She looks for a safe place—somewhere to put the money. She takes the bills out of her handbag and then decides to wrap them in the *Los Angeles Times*. Then she hears a voice, coming in at the window Norman opened.

It is the voice of a woman, an old woman even—yet it is strong enough to carry from the house. "No! I tell you no! I won't have you bringing strange young girls in here for supper—by candlelight, I suppose, in the cheap, erotic fashion of young men with cheap, erotic minds?"

Norman's voice tries to respond, "Mother, she's just a stranger!"

But "Mother's" voice settles everything with prim wordplay: "I refuse to speak of disgusting things, because they disgust me! Do you understand, boy?"

Norman appears, downcast, like a servant, carrying a tray with milk and sandwiches. "My mother isn't quite herself today," he apologizes to Marion. It is the first clear moment in the film that gets respect the first time we see it and a guffaw the second. And it is a sly hint to us all that those people who share the fun of wordplay may be driving this story. More than that, it is a moment when a film exerting a fierce grip on us alludes to the possibility of being artificial as well as terrifying.

This point needs more discussion, for it is vital. Alfred Hitchcock was always a self-conscious craftsman making his films. He had an early taste for "private" jokes; his cameo appearances grew out of that. It was a way of saying "Look, it's me" or "I did this" in the midst of a story (a suspension of disbelief) that is supposed to be complete. Movies—comedies especially—had been prone to such winks at the audience before: Groucho and Cary Grant both seem to arch an eyebrow at the camera from time to time, as if to say, "Get me out of here." But in general, that "here" in movies—the story and its place—was sacrosanct. Pictures did not allude to their own making or process.

But now consider Vladimir Nabokov's *Lolita*, first published in 1955. Quite early in that novel, Humbert Humbert (or is it Nabokov himself?) steps out of the story to advise us, "You can always count on a murderer for a fancy style." That's a fair comment in that *Lolita* is a book about a criminal in which the language has the radiance of triumphal confession. And it's a gesture to the elegant slaughter to which Hitchcock always aspired—a sort of killing that even the victim might appreciate. But "fancy" also carries connotations of "show-off" or "gay." And in American films of the '30s, '40s, and '50s, mannered, high-gloss style was often code for homosexuality. Think of Waldo Lydecker (Clifton Webb) in *Laura* or Casper Gutman (Sydney Greenstreet) in *The Maltese Falcon*.

The use of wordplay in the mother's offstage voice in *Psycho* seems to me the same kind of thing (the voice was that of actor Paul Jasmin, a friend of Anthony Perkins). To say the least, it is theatrical and literary—and very far from what an old woman might say in rural California. It is the voice of an authored character, and that leads us to this point—that coming to his first great climax in *Psycho*, Hitchcock could not find another voice than the one that both admits and revels in duality. So he is teasing the first audience and congratulating the second. Above all, he is owning up to the idea that a film (or a book) is a game to be played as opposed to a dream to be inhabited. The early Arizonan naturalism of our story is gone. We are in legend or mythology. We are in a work of art. And the artist feels compelled to own up.

IN THE PARLOR

Norman is not quite sure where to offer supper. There's his office, but "eating in an office is just too officious," so they go back into his parlor. If this is Norman's room or home (and we will find no such place in the house), then it may remind us of the storeroom behind the hardware store where Sam Loomis makes his wifeless "home."

Norman's parlor is old-fashioned and undistinguished, but it is an aviary for stuffed birds. These figures are the more alarming in that they throw shadows on the ceiling—and they can only do that with a lighting scheme that is scarcely natural or domestic. So this room is theater, too, and the function of theater surely narrows its gaze when Norman tells Marion (picking at her sandwich), "You eat like a bird." "You'd know," she replies, looking at the taxidermy. "No, not really," says Norman. "Anyway, I hear the expression 'eats like a bird' is really a falsity"—and he stammers over that word. The stammer is the last decorative bow on the costume called "shyness," and it is something Marion feels. Norman likes her. He is attracted to her. But there is something in his life that holds him back from a candid exploration of the attraction.

The conversation allows Norman to tell us about himself, and a pattern sets in—in the script, in the direction, but in Perkins himself. He is an alarming mixture of meekness and anger. He stuffs birds. It is his hobby. He sits back in his chair telling Marion, who is smart and interested enough to realize she is with a disturbed personality, one who makes her want to confess. He asks where she is going, and she says she's looking for a private island. Norman gets it. He starts to talk about "private traps": "And none of us can ever get out. We scratch and claw, but only at the air, only at each other. And for all of it we never budge an inch." He stares. The camera angle on him shifts from three-quarters on in a full shot to profile in a closer shot. Hitchcock is telling us that Norman's disturbed.

But as soon as we feel that, Perkins gives one of his deprecating chuckles or boyish smiles. He knows, too, doesn't he? He's got it under control. The conversation deepens, and it becomes a matter of crosscut close-ups. Yes, his mother insults him and bullies him, but she's "ill"—her husband, his father, died, and then another man came along who talked her into building the motel and

then he died, too. It was all a terrible strain on her. With
only a son left.

Marion and Norman are friends now—and we realize
again how little friendship there has been in the picture.
She wonders if his mother could be "put . . . someplace."
"A madhouse?" he asks, and now he looks like a ghost in
looming close-up. He couldn't do that, he says. It would
be like burying her. "I don't hate her. I hate what she has
become. I hate her illness."

Marion apologizes for sounding uncaring, and Norman
arrives at the line that—in a way—concludes the film: "We
all go a little mad sometimes. Haven't you?" And Marion,
or Janet, breaks into a lovely and even a loving smile. It is
as if her trap has been opened or relaxed. It is as if this
strange conversation—and there is hardly anything like it
in American film—has helped her see the folly of what she
has done. She decides to repair the mistake. "I'd like to go
back and try to pull myself out of it," she says. And she
says, back to Phoenix.

Norman says he'll bring her breakfast in the morning.
She admits her real name—Marion Crane. She goes to her
cabin.

One needs to see this scene several times to catch all the
nuances and to appreciate how much it is the most ordi-

nary, natural, and kindly event in the picture as well as the most searching. Norman doesn't know Marion's "crime" or folly, but he has an uncanny sense of how people can go wrong and ruin their own lives. He has simply proposed a way of avoiding the worst traps, but his philosophy is foreboding, and it hovers between being earned experience and neurotic anxiety. In some respects, he has told her what Sam might have said—if he'd been asked. Be sensible; return the money. Grow up. He has freed her, and it's not out of the range of cinematic logic that the next morning he might ask if he could go along with her. He might even indicate that he had feelings for her. She could say she has a boyfriend already—but if she didn't admit that, then we'd know why. Because Norman has moved her.

But hasn't he also given hints of danger? Of course. But is it a danger any greater than Marion's yielding to the reckless idea of going off with the money? The possibility has been reached—in screen chemistry—that these two people might help each other. And Hitchcock, in his time, made important films based on the idea of emotional rescue (*Rebecca, Spellbound, Notorious, North by Northwest*) as well as some where the rescue attempt is disastrous (*Vertigo*).

SILENT CINEMA

Hitchcock began in the silent era, of course, and he never wavered in his fondness for passages of "pure cinema" in which the pictures tell us everything. As Marion goes to her cabin, Norman prowls the office: he smiles at her fake name in the register; he stands close to his stuffed birds. And then he takes a painting off the wall—it is an eighteenth-century study of a rape—to reveal a spy hole through which he can see the interior of cabin 1.

We see what he sees. Marion, undressing, down to her black underwear, in front of the bathroom. We see a big close-up of his eye watching. We see her turn toward the bathroom. He backs away from the spy hole.

He is troubled, angry, trying to be brave. He looks up toward the house, and his jutting jaw seems to say that he is going to give his mother a piece of his mind. He walks up to the house. For the first time, we see its interior—lavish, with potted plants, a huge staircase, and a banister post as big as Norman. He is about to go upstairs, but then he weakens and instead walks beside the staircase, his hands in his pockets. There is a room at the end of the corridor, and he sits down there at a table, hunched up in his loneliness. It is one of the most poignant pictures of solitude in all of Hitchcock's work.

In cabin 1, Marion is sitting at a table. She does a sum that hardly speaks well of her education: $40,000 minus $700. I'll leave the answer to you. In fact, this is visual storytelling that was archaic by 1959. But the scrap of paper is important. She takes the paper, goes into the bathroom, and flushes it down the toilet.

Yes, you know what a toilet is, but in 1960, apparently, the sight and sound of it in operation in a movie were shocking.

She takes off her robe. She steps into the shower. This is the moment.

3

Room Service

PSYCHO HAS RUN ABOUT FORTY MINUTES. A crime has been committed, though a naive one, without malice or much damage, and we will learn later that its victims are prepared to press no charges, so long as the missing money is restored. There has been no overt violence, though a lot of harsh or unkind words have been exchanged. More or less, the film has been intent on presenting the portrait of a woman, Marion Crane, who does a stupid thing and learns that she needs to make amends for it. The film likes her. It catches her relief when she comes to her moment of critical self-awareness. But at the same time, the process of film—the objective scrutiny, the thing that says, "Look at her"—has been the engine for a mounting tension. And now that tension is going to be let loose, or be rewarded.

In 1960, for sure, filmgoers had reason to expect rules and reliable indicators. And so, from the first moments of *Psycho*, it is clear that Janet Leigh is the star of the film. Her actions make the plot of the film, and she (or what she sees) is on-screen nearly all the time. Yet the credits of the film read, "Starring Anthony Perkins, John Gavin, and Vera Miles"—and Miss Miles has not yet appeared. Then at the end of the cast list, the screen warns us, "And Janet Leigh as Marion Crane." That was a way of saying that Leigh's participation was not quite central or dominant, and might even be a bright, short-lived cameo.

It's hard to know how carefully anyone read those credits, let alone understood them. It's certain, I think, that by the time we reach the Bates Motel we reckon ourselves on board a Janet Leigh vehicle. Yet one factor argues against that. For Leigh, or Marion, has been steadily spied on. Three times in forty minutes we have seen her in her brassiere. More than that (much more), her attractiveness or vulnerability has been sharpened by her "naughtiness," her willful escape from reality or responsibility, which we have seen in every detail. I think there is an underlying psychological urge in us, the audience, to see her stripped and ravished, to see her rebuked. In part, that comes from a study of Hitchcock's films where the close inspection of distressed women eroticizes them, and because Hitchcock always had this readiness for male punishment (you can see it explored in *Notorious*, *Under Capricorn*, and *Dial M for Murder*—you can feel it nearly everywhere).

By 1960 Hitchcock was many things: a very skilled director of suspense situations, a witty explorer of character and situation, and an analyst of his own medium, a man who was entranced by the way film's mechanics could manipulate audiences and play on their feelings of fear and desire. So we are afraid for Marion Crane, in case she is caught or exposed, yet we want her, too—in the sense that we want her exposed further to our desire. You can hardly consider the first section of *Psycho* as anything other than an exploration of the process of voyeurism—the building of sexual excitement through watching.

Thus, it's important to see that what happens—the shower murder—is both stunningly unexpected and a logical release of the pressures built up in the long, sustained overture. Orgasm at last.

That explosion takes the form of removing our most beloved character and the apparent star of the film in one frenzy of violence—perhaps the most violent passage until then in American film. There's no doubt that Hitchcock was intrigued by that drastic authority. It was a way of saying that his design was more important than film's commercial habits or structure.

But something else has to be said: the film so far is the fairly plain description of a series of grinding processes — postcoital wistfulness, several sniping conversations, driving and pursuit, ordeal and fatigue, and then the action at the motel and the way Marion seems to have bumped into a kindred spirit and a kind soul. In the first forty minutes we see things happen. In the next few minutes we see their hysterical suggestion made flesh. And that is because the picture represents a crossroads moment when a great rift appeared in the thing called censorship.

The movies had always been based on a tension. On the one hand, the form says, "Look, I can show you something you have never seen before": it could be an act of violence, a sexual suggestion; it might be a beautiful man or woman alone with their thoughts, unaware of being spied on. Much of the charm of pictures lay in this privileged opportunity granted to us. For instance, do you want to look at Garbo or Harlow at your leisure so that you can speculate over whether they are wearing underwear? Here you are. At the same time, the business apparatus of movies was always backed up by a guardian-like sternness that said, "Don't expect to get a look at truly secret things. Don't think we're going to let Garbo or Harlow take off the dress—that outer cover—so that you can see whether you were right or wrong. Yes, we'll show you 'murder,' but don't expect us to be cruel or bloodthirsty or murderous about it. Because that would be too naughty—and would put film too close to sadism or torture."

No country lives as blithely or as uneasily with the opposed ideals of orgy and restriction as America. No other country has such warring impulses toward libertarianism and restraint. No other country required so detailed or comical a code of what could be seen on public screens and what could not. And no other film business so encouraged the ingenuity of directors, photographers, and actors to see what they could get away with.

Hitchcock had approached *Psycho* as a test in that special area. I suspect that his interest in the story of the film was always secondary to his fascination with whether he could get certain things past the censorship code—the first postcoital scene, the nagging sexual scrutiny, the flushing of the piece of paper with the calculation, and what happens in the shower. There had never been a scene so blunt, or so drab, as that sexual-aftermath opening. Apparently, in all of American film, there had never been a scene that showed a toilet being flushed before—it really is quite exhilarating to see what tender creatures we were in 1960. And there had never been a murder carried out in such detail, with nakedness, repeated violence, and so much blood. So it was a fair contest: Hitchcock against the system. And we have seen how much this matter of "taste" worked to separate Hitch from Paramount, the studio at which he had made his great films of the 1950s.

Of course, Hitch had another challenge in the sequence: he had to make us think we had seen one character commit the murder while in truth another did it. It is predatory genius, therefore, to show the blurred outline of a tall woman coming toward the shower through the curtain. It is "perfect" cinema to have the upraised knife and the scream in Herrmann's strings. But it is pure convenience to have the killer in close-up, with dark on his face—as if the bathroom has not already been established as a furnace of light. But we are so afraid on first viewing, and so startled by what does happen, that we do not question the photographic logic of that close-up. The silhouette of Mother is so daunting and arresting—and Marion does not seem to recognize the man she has been talking to.

Hitchcock separated this filming from the rest of the shoot, just as he knew that acceptance of the edited whole would require a campaign. But it's worth stressing that his reputation on the eve of *Psycho* was that of an English connoisseur of mystery stories. He was not regarded as a man of violence—in the way of, say, Samuel Fuller, Anthony Mann, Nicholas Ray, Robert Aldrich, or other American directors who dealt in combat and conflict. In *Rear Window*, for example, we never saw the killing. In *North by Northwest*, the crop-duster sequence was as comic or absurd as it was frightening. There is very little direct violence in *Vertigo* or *The Wrong Man*, in *Notorious*, *Rebecca*, or *Suspicion*. In *The Trouble with Harry* there is a corpse, but we are schooled to regard it as a source of humor. There is a great strangling in *Strangers on a Train*—Bruno Anthony killing Guy Haynes's wife and then handing the corpse down to us (like a gift). There are pieces of suspense, like the slowly tearing sleeve in *Saboteur* before Norman Lloyd will plunge down from the Statue of Liberty. There is a claustrophobic image of drowning in *Foreign Correspondent*. But in general, the killing in a Hitchcock film had been an opportunity for artistry or artifice—things that diluted the shock impact.

Don't misunderstand me. There was always an odd current of violence in Hitchcock—I think of a moment in *To Catch a Thief* (a sunny film) when Jessie Royce Landis stubs out a cigarette in an untouched fried egg. Still, there is nothing in Hitchcock's work prior to *Psycho* to match the wounding of James Stewart's hand in *The Man from Laramie*, the knife fight in *Rebel Without a Cause*, or the strutting violence of Mike Hammer in *Kiss Me Deadly*. Hitch conducted himself like a very plump man with more taste for wicked thoughts than ugly deeds.

As he prepared *Psycho*, he often referred his crew members to the French film *Les Diaboliques*, made by Henri-Georges Clouzot in 1955 (and taken from a novel by the team that wrote *Vertigo*). This is a story in which an adulterous couple tries to frighten the wife to death by exposing her weak heart to scenes of increasing horror. It is effective and macabre and a literal acting out of Hitch's urge to impose terror through "pure film."

But he was also a master of detail, and clearly the shower sequence was to be the most thoroughly and extensively premeditated and designed scene in his work to that time. The shower scene was filmed just days before Christmas, December 17–23, 1959. In the event, seventy-eight pieces of film would make a forty-five-second sequence. As much as ever, Hitchcock had storyboarded the whole thing, shot by shot, and he seems to have kept title designer Saul Bass present, in case he had need of more advice. Janet Leigh was present most of the time, and she recalled working in a skin-colored moleskin, without any nude figure. But another stand-in, Marli Renfro, was used, too, so that Leigh never had to work in the nude. As for "Mother," Anthony Perkins was excused. A stuntwoman named Margo Epper did all his and her shots—was this a way of shielding Perkins from the cruelty of his alter ego?

I ask that question because it's proper to wonder whether Perkins's Norman—so carefully built up in the seven or eight minutes of prior screen time—is actually capable of the onslaught that follows. Norman in the office gives off alarming signals, to be sure. He has a dark vision. But his kindness and tolerance are also palpable. In other words, the film's cockamamie inner fallacy—that Mother can take Norman over—is under real threat just because of all the fond details in Perkins's performance. There is nothing in this awkward young man that suggests the anger of Mother—the repeated thrusts with the blade. Rather, the energy and the malice come more from the film's design than from Norman's psychotic state.

This is a profound point—despite the terror in *Psycho* at first and the fun that comes later: Does any one of us really believe in Mother's power to possess her son? Or are we close to the point of admitting that this picture does violence for its own sake, and as a way of fulfilling our voyeuristic pact with its stealth and its gradual pressure? In other words, is the moment of *Psycho* a true revelation of human nature or a threshold in filmmaking that says let violence run riot and to hell with the consequences? Was fear its subject, more than psychosis? That might begin to account for why, allegedly, Janet Leigh and many viewers of the film began to feel more doubtful about the use of showers (than about their use of mothers?).

The fact that Norman and Mother were crucially not represented in the shooting is one sign of the stress on technique (the scene is less acted than edited and composed). But another is the way in which the crew was able to reappraise the shower material as the execution of an elaborate plan. For the sake of argument, suppose that in another way of doing things, Mother/Norman comes quietly and silently up to the shower stall. Suppose we see the terrible look of anticipation and apprehension on Norman's face. And then suppose we feel Norman move forward, gently, and slide the knife into an unsuspecting body. Suppose we see that penetration as well as the look on Norman's face—to be followed by an agony of collision and outrage that then turns into the frenzy of stabbing. Or suppose that one stroke of the knife accomplishes murder.

That at least attempts to make the mind process in Mother/Norman dramatically credible, but it delivers a quite appalling moment of premeditated violence (applied like a kiss) that would never have got past the censor in 1960—and would have destroyed the remainder of the film. Make no mistake, even if the murder occurred halfway through the film, there was a balance in *Psycho* that required another hour of screen time, an hour that is as fabricated and spurious as the first hour is solid and resonant.

Those days in a motel bathroom were all a matter of precise camera angling, of showing nudity so briefly that it did not register as lewdness, of filming knife thrusts in so fragmentary a form that no blade ever pierced skin (though some gourmets have slowed the film on a Moviola and believe they can see the bulge of a blood drop). Later, Hitchcock would be piously boastful about this "restraint," and one can hear him lecturing the censors in the same tone. "Ladies and gentlemen, a knife falls. We then see blood burst from a body. But why am I or my film to be blamed for that sequence and our fancying that we have seen a wound?" Why is he to be blamed when all he used was chocolate sauce? The piety is less than warming or admirable. It's too close to the technical pride taken by gas-chamber engineers and too removed from the plain and undeniable impact of that work.

There's another point: because of the way it is shown, the murder is far more what happens to Marion (the rebuke visited upon her) than the lyrical expression of the killer and murderous impulse. It's murder set free, kicked into ignition, without any encumbrance or muffling from shame. It's not nearly enough to argue that "Mother" needs to kill to stifle Norman's lust, or even to satisfy her revenge. Who are we kidding? This killing is passionate. This killer comes.

Yet the film is called *Psycho*, and when all is said and done it is the story of a psychotic or aberrant killer. Marion Crane has been beautifully set up, but her destiny now materializes as a force violently altered by the dynamic of a chance meeting. It is not her fault what happens; it is far out of proportion as a reward or a rebuke. She is an atom bumped into by another atom, and thus she has to go. Hitchcock had been fascinated by chance meetings (crisscross) ever since *Strangers on a Train*. What appealed to him especially in Joseph Stefano's screenplay was the sheer bad luck of a naughty girl being caught up in a storm so much bigger than herself. And what underlines this silly luck is the way Norman—in cleaning up the room after the killing—does not even notice the stolen money, let alone take it for himself. One miniaturist passes another in the night.

And so, the shower sequence is a bizarre duel between what is visible and what is not. In fact, the imaginary triumphs over the actual (as is usually so with Hitchcock), and the audience is left to make sense of the gap between the ordinary and the absurd (the life on the road versus life at the Bates house). There's no doubt about the cinematic quality of the shower sequence. This is an old-fashioned montage, an impression of lethal attack, to which has been added the utmost expressiveness of Herrmann's music and the soundtrack in which it is embedded. The total effect is delirium—a finely wrought madness in which all the elements are tortured taste. The question that remains is not just who has killed Marion Crane, but what tempest has felt bound to overtake the film? The answer is the same— the director, and the reason for both answers is, "To keep this hysterical film alive."

Every shot in the crushed minute is "beautiful" but strained to breaking point. I include in this the several shots of Marion (head and shoulders) posed in the water stream like an angel in heavenly light; the blurred, out-of-focus shots of Marion intruded upon; the thrashing blows; the agonized face; the darkness coming to the flow of water; the beautiful shots of Marion's face, fainting away, as she begins to slide down the tiled wall; the rasp of the shower curtain; the drain in the shower stall that becomes like an eye (or the ultimate sexual orifice) in close-up; and then the last shot, the zoom away from Marion's head, collapsed and squashed against the bathroom floor—the shot that gave so much trouble and which became a subject of special pride for Hitchcock.

THE CUTTING OF THE shower sequence was just a prelude in the battle Hitchcock could expect with the Production Code officials. The fate of a movie in those days depended on how it was handled by the Code officials, and Hitchcock was hopeful of his perilous position. Frank Freeman was still in a chief liaison position between the producers and the Code office, and the real force at the Code was Geoffrey Shurlock, an Englishman, only a few years older than Hitch. Shurlock had taken his job in 1954, and he and Hitch had had good relations on everything from *Rear Window* to *North by Northwest*, pictures famous for their "tasteful" double meanings and sexual innuendo. (In

To Catch a Thief, Grace Kelly takes Cary Grant on a picnic. Looking at the cold chicken, she asks him whether he'd prefer a leg or a breast. You decide, he says. And Shurlock had been prepared to let the audience enjoy that point.)

Shurlock is generally regarded as a man who helped liberalize the Code's enforcement, but on a film like *Psycho* he was not just the enemy in advance but a door that needed to be worked and oiled. Hitch had established an amiable, sophisticated relationship with Shurlock. He knew enough to flatter the censor and to let him feel that they were men of the world, who understood dirty jokes, say, in a way that helped excuse them. It was calculated, and Shurlock was at liberty to see how he was being used. Equally, the history of such moral guardians is that they were proud of being taken seriously and given an inside view of the picture business.

Hitch had always figured on three main areas of dispute with the Code: the opening scene, the flushing toilet, and the shower murder. In the first case, he preached plot point. He had to have the right to establish the situation between these two people. The scene was frank, yes (in fact it wasn't), though nothing really happened and the audience got the point.

As for the toilet, well, it was crucial as a plot link: it was only finding the slip of paper in the toilet bowl that proved Marion had been at the motel. Beyond that, Hitch could surmise that the average American flushed a toilet half a dozen times a day without having conniption fits. It wasn't as if anyone in the film used the bathroom as plumbing intended (and that taboo has hardly yet been broken fifty years later).

As far as the shower was concerned, Hitchcock was as cunning as could be. The editing was so fast, it was very hard to know what had been seen. And it was not fair to run the scene in slow-motion, because no one would ever see it that way. Time and again, Hitchcock made his plea—that no sexual nudity was evident, that no blade pierced flesh. And, plainly, the scene was vital. Furthermore, Hitch had a trump card. That big shot of Marion tipped over the edge of the bath, with her buttocks showing—a fearsome shot but a thing of beauty—well, that was negotiable. In fact, Hitch had shot it and put it in his cut as a tool to be withdrawn later if the Code would pass the rest—the film Hitch had seen. It's clear from their notes that the Code functionaries were confused: they couldn't be sure what they had seen—and they were being lectured about "reaction" by one of the greatest film and audience experts ever.

They caved in. Like most figures in their position, they felt a mounting gap between what was allowed in cinema and what audiences found acceptable. They passed the film, and the Catholic League of Decency slid away from a crisis with a "B"—"morally objectionable in part for all."

That was less than fifty years ago. It's not that *Psycho* didn't shock many people and didn't acquire a reputation for cynical sensationalism. Still, the real measure of the breakthrough that had occurred—in the name of pure cinema—is in the bloodletting, sadism, and slaughter that are now taken for granted. In terms of the cruelties we no longer notice, we are another species.

4

Housekeeping

MOTHER'S HELPER

WHAT FOLLOWS THE MURDER and its shock is a prolonged scene of restoration in which the pace and the meticulous detail are as calming as the entire cleansing process. From that shot of Marion half in the shower stall, half spread against the floor, we cut to a view of the house, its windows burning. And now we hear Norman's voice, "Mother! Oh, God! Mother, mother! Blood, blood!" And soon we see the figure of Norman running from the house. He enters cabin 1 and is appalled, nauseated, stricken. His large hand covers his mouth.

And then, like the sorcerer's apprentice, he puts the wrecked place back together again. It is another sustained passage of silent cinema—if you forget Herrmann's quiet, assisting, sympathetic music. It is a long scene in which an actor simply does things. There is no talk; there is very little in the way of reflection or inward aside. Yet it may be the best stuff Perkins delivers in the picture, for to understand his perfection in the scene you have to know not just how far you are being tricked but how innately obedient and tidy-minded he is.

Of course, we are at the start of a fairly lengthy second half of a movie in which Hitch wants us to stay ready to be surprised again. But first calm must be restored. No matter that several clues make it clear what has happened. Seconds after what may be the most lavish assault and outrage in American film, the ripples of murder are stilled by a lengthy cleanup operation, enough to be able to say, "Look, nothing happened." And we are reassured by the process: we begin to trust that there is not another demon coming out of the wall, and we begin to like Norman—even if cleaning up after this "Mother" is only going to intensify the mess of his life. To escape the unbearable, we need to trust Norman, and so we fall for the defense that he is his mother's helpless helper.

We watch Norman now as we watched Marion earlier. In a couple of shots that wad of money folded up inside the *Los Angeles Times* is evident, yet Norman never notices it. Almost by habit, he goes to his office and collects a mop and a bucket. Does he know how to do this? He takes the dead body and wraps it in the shower curtain (never let a prop go to waste in a tightly budgeted film). He washes the blood off his hands—we notice, along with Hitchcock, that Norman, or Perkins, has uncommonly long fingers. Artistic hands.

He washes out the shower stall. There is a shot of the sodden mop swinging down its length. He collects Marion's slippers and her towels. He brings her Ford close to the cabin and loads the body in the trunk. He gets her luggage and her clothes. He takes a last look around and sees the newspaper. He picks it up but never notices the money, and he tosses it with everything else into the trunk.

He drives the car to the nearby swamp. The morning light is coming up as he eases the vehicle down into the mud. It starts to sink. We see him watching, munching on small candy. Then the car halts, and his jaw stops. We are with him—we want it to sink. We want oblivion. Then the mud starts to work again. I wonder how far Hitchcock the ironist smiled that this extra "flushing" shot was never noticed by the censors. After all, the white Ford goes into the black mud, with gulping sounds, too, like life passing into a sump of shit. The swamp has not been referred to before—it is just there, like the great stratum of sewage in the world. Of course, seen in those terms, the car being sucked away is repellently suggestive, all of which proves that censors may notice the lightest things first.

As the car sinks, a flicker of a grin crosses the face of this gaunt country boy—poor Norman! The things he has to be ready for. What a blessing for him that he has such a domestic fusspot as his director, a man who—magnificent in violence—would still harbor such a deep respect for restoration and order.

There's an extra but characteristic irony in that the core of the film should be an outrage followed by meticulous re-ordering. Yet this is true to Hitchcock in so many ways. In word and deed, he was a scrupulously law-abiding man. The story he told of being briefly incarcerated in a police cell as a child (by his father) carried a warning that lasted a lifetime. The police are often menacing figures in his work, and he nursed the subject of the falsely accused person—as if it had a primal sadomasochistic appeal. He lived and worked in an orderly middle-class way, yet he was persistently drawn to illegal actions and secret guilt. Think of Maxim in *Rebecca*, Scottie in *Vertigo*, Alicia in *Notorious*, the woman in *Under Capricorn*—the anguish of these characters is always a guilty secret and a kind of suppressed breakdown. *Psycho* is simply the most direct treatment of this thesis, with Jekyll and Hyde as mother and son.

LILA

In the script for *Psycho*, the last of the Ford sinking into the swamp cuts to a shot inside the house in which Norman finds a pile of bloody clothes and shoes outside Mother's room and disposes of it. Such a scene would emphasize the existence of Mother, but it only repeats the gist of the long cleanup sequence, and it may have been deemed a mistake to go inside the house too soon, or too casually. After all, the house is about to become the ultimate taboo place. But deleting the clothes serves another purpose: it allows the film to move to Sam in his hardware store in Fairvale writing a letter to Marion, urging that they make up their minds to live together.

This letter's request is urgent, yet Sam does not telephone Marion to hasten the decision. This underlines the lack of immediacy in the Sam-Marion relationship. But it also leaves us wondering why the couple weren't living together ages ago. "So what if we're poor and cramped and miserable?" Sam writes. "At least we'll be happy." In fact, Sam has yielded on the alleged problem of poverty that prompted Marion's act of theft. Tacitly, it suggests that the whole trap she enters has been made by Sam's emotional reluctance—he will not take the plunge with the woman he says he loves because he is financially insecure. In a way, Hitchcock is disowning the first part of the film while leaving us with the impression that Sam is not really that desirable a husband. Could he ever talk to her the way Norman does in that brief supper, first and last?

From Sam's letter (being written at his desk in the living room at the back of the store), we cut to a middle-aged woman in the store purchasing insect repellent—it guarantees to kill every insect, she notes, but is it painless? "And I say—insect or man—death should always be painless." On that line (ironic? teasing? or part of the undergrowth of hypocrisy established earlier in the film?), Marion's sister, Lila (Vera Miles), enters the Loomis Hardware Store. Lila is young and moderately attractive, yet Miles plays the part without warmth or grace. As it stands, her subdued toughness is not a useful contribution to the film so much as a sign that Hitchcock has hardly the time to make more of her. She is suspicious. She has come to Fairvale to sort out the matter. She will become, with Sam, one of the inquiring agents who unravel the final mystery. But she is never as

likable as Marion, not as warm or sexy, not as amused. She
is a drag and a numb place. Does she represent a family in
which Marion might feel chilled or alienated?

I put it that way because this situation might have been
greatly expanded. Suppose that Lila is not Marion's sister
but her mother—she could be just under sixty, she could
be a character, and she could be an emotionally dominating
force who (once we see her) we recognize as Marion's
problem in life. If you want a better sense of how such a
character could have been portrayed, just think of the
mother (Jessica Tandy) in Hitchcock's next film, *The
Birds*. That mother could have sustained the emotional life
of *Psycho* in ways that are simply overlooked. She could
have been a presence who began to see weakness in Sam.
For instance, there is a shop assistant in the hardware
store. Suppose that assistant was a pretty girl, a light-
weight, but still you can see that the complacent Sam is
two-timing Marion with her. The earlier hint that the
"love" between Sam and Marion is less than intense could
come to mean so much more. That portrayal would bring
more tragedy to Marion's story because it would let us see
that this mother has never granted Marion her indepen-
dence in life.

DETECTIVE

Then Arbogast (Martin Balsam) appears—and literally so. He is a full-frontal face, in close-up first and then big close-up, forcing himself into the film and into the meeting between Sam and Lila (the first, we notice). In some ways, Arbogast fits in with the gallery of small male parts in the film—pushy, tough, questioning, and far from sentimental. In time, he warms up: Martin Balsam was a very appealing actor, hard to hold at a distance for long. Still, Arbogast is introduced as an abrasive force—albeit fresh blood that the movie needs at this moment. Not that the emotional center of the film shifts. It was with Marion first, and then Norman took on the load. Lila and Arbogast, arriving late, are never endearing, and Sam remains a cold, rather unpleasant man. As it emerges that Marion is dead, he shows so little grief. I can't see how he and Marion were going to be happy.

Arbogast is a private detective, hired by Lowery in Phoenix to find the money. He's had this sort of case before, and he can't resist the assumption that if a pretty girl and $40,000 are missing, then they're likely together. But he allows in a rather patronizing way that he doubts Sam had anything to do with it. So he proposes to make a tour of local hotels, motels, and rooming houses to see if he can trace Marion's path.

He tries a handful of places before he drives up to the office of the Bates Motel where Norman is sitting on the veranda with a handful of candies. Arbogast admits he nearly missed the place, and Norman blames himself—"I'm always forgetting to turn the sign on." That is credible behavior. As a motel drops out of use, you would forget to turn the sign on. But when Marion appeared out of the night, Norman said he had forgotten to turn the sign *off*. So didn't he turn it on as bait for some tired traveler?

A scene follows between Arbogast and Norman of sparring, inquiring talk, with the private eye being fended off. There's a story that when they filmed it, Balsam and Perkins were so quick on their cues and made such a deft scene that the crew gave them a standing ovation. And it's talk at which the detective is so much more adept. Norman falters. He makes mistakes. He leaves clues that Arbogast snaps up. In a quiet way, Norman is now the hounded one, and if we really want his guilty secret protected, then maybe we are on his side. But if a part of us is guessing the very far-fetched truth, then the scene plays as a dance. For myself, I enjoy it in the way the crew might have—seeing Mr. Tongue-tied and Mr. Glib play a fast set.

Arbogast gets Norman to say no one has stayed at the motel lately. Then he contradicts himself. And Norman has to show him the register—and there is "Marie Samuels" in Marion Crane's writing. There's an astonishing low-angle shot of Norman trying to look at the name—from directly below, his jaw still munching, predatory yet vulnerable, too. And again you feel Hitchcock teasing us, as if to say, "This would be a lot easier if you'd only see the truth." Arbogast shows a picture. Norman starts stammering. We're in crosscut big close-ups by now, and Arbogast is nearly stroking the story out of the helpless youth—you can see that Arbogast would be a very good cop. He nods at the answers and says, "If it doesn't jell, it isn't aspic. And this ain't jelling."

They go outside, and Arbogast detects a hesitation in Norman over cabin 1. Then he looks up at the house and sees a figure at a window. That's when Norman admits his mother is there. Arbogast asks to talk to her. But Norman won't have it. There's nearly a conflict, and Norman asks him to leave. But Norman must know the game is up—this Arbogast has guessed too much and caught Norman in too many mistakes.

Arbogast goes to a phone, calls the hardware store, reports what he's learned, and says he's going to try to see Mrs. Bates. He'll be about an hour.

Arbogast is a blessing, so beautifully played that he obscures his own redundancy. Hitchcock has a mystery waiting for an answer. He must know the answer is feeble or inadequate to the great trauma that has occurred. Arbogast is spinning out screen time in a very artful way. Here comes his great moment, as fussy and as empty as the man himself.

STAIRCASE

He drives back to the motel. No one is in sight, so he makes his way up to the house. As he comes in the front door, he takes off his fedora hat—it is a nice touch but exposes his baldness. He sees the great staircase leading up. He sees Norman's den at the end of the back corridor. Hat in hand, he begins to ascend the staircase. The camera rises with him, but ahead of him, and climbs to the top corner of the upstairs hall. Only then does a side door open on the upper floor. A female figure appears. We cannot see her face, but we look directly down as this figure, knife upraised, meets Arbogast at the top of the stairs. The knife plunges. Blood jumps up on Arbogast's face.

He begins to fall backward, but it is a rather awkward, rigged shot. He falls, but he is clearly in a chair, gesticulating, and that shot is mixed with a downward tracking shot. He falls on his back, and the female figure is on him, the knife striking repeatedly, urged on by Herrmann's music. It is the end of Arbogast, and it is Hitchcock at his best and worst, simultaneously.

The staircase is a place of stress and ordeal in Hitchcock—you could say he made that terrain perilous long before he took on the shower stall. Cary Grant has to save Ingrid Bergman in *Notorious* by bringing her down the staircase. Farley Granger seeks out Robert Walker's father at the top of a staircase guarded by a mastiff in *Strangers on a Train*. In *The Birds*, Tippi Hedren will have to go upstairs to the attic. *To Catch a Thief* is all heights and rooftops. And then there is *Vertigo* and the idea of a man suffering from that condition electing to live in San Francisco.

The staircase crane shot in *Psycho* is very beautiful. Hitch was as good on stairs as he was with agonized faces. It can be defended, I suppose, as being vital to information concealment. At ground level, we would have to see Mother's face. But when felicities of style exist to conceal information, then they are in great danger of becoming baroque and decadent. It is style for style's sake, a trap not entirely buried by the pumping of that knife and the frenzy of the music. Above all, the killing of Arbogast evokes no sympathy for him. He is just the figure in a tour de force execution. The virtuoso crane shot is all on the side of the killer—though designed to get the best view of his cruelty.

So the Bates house has now assumed diabolical powers. It is a place where reality can be manipulated for murderous ends.

PERIWINKLE BLUE

Sam and Lila are still waiting in the hardware store: bored yet anxious, they make a grim picture of any loving couple trying to live there—Hitchcock photographs the place with heavy stress on the blades and weapons of gardening implements. It is not a cozy site.

Sam determines to visit the motel. When he gets there he finds no one, but Norman—at the swamp, tending his plantings—hears Sam calling out for Arbogast and knows his peace is over. In the middle of the night, Sam and Lila call on Fairvale's sheriff, Al Chambers. In dressing gowns, he and his wife come downstairs to greet the distraught couple. Chambers is John McIntire, his wife Lurene Tuttle. Putting McIntire in the film now is like doubling up on Martin Balsam, for these are two very amiable supporting players, figures of trust. Moreover, McIntire was fifty-three and looked older—he had been around, and he was likely as old as Fairvale.

He and his wife listen to the story. They exchange glances at the mention of the old woman. Chambers calls the Bates Motel and talks to Norman. He says Norman admitted that Arbogast called, but said he had left. The wry sheriff tells them all, "Norman Bates's mother has been dead and buried in Greenlawn Cemetery for the past ten years!" Mrs. Chambers adds that she picked out the dress the woman was buried in—periwinkle blue. No, the color doesn't matter, but the quaint word in this woman's voice is a perfect example of Hitchcock's macabre comedy. It's a reaching out for gentility and prettiness in a world where the blood is black.

Ten years before Mrs. Bates had poisoned her lover when she found he had someone else, and then she killed herself. It was a famous case. "Norman found them dead together," supplies the sheriff's wife. "In bed." Sam and Lila insist that Mrs. Bates is alive. "Well," says Chambers, "if the woman up there is Mrs. Bates, who's that woman buried out in Greenlawn Cemetery?"

WHAT WOULD YOU DO?

The closer mystery comes to explanation, the nearer it is to destroying itself. That threat hangs over a great deal of suspense cinema. To put it very simply: you can suggest that something lurks at the end of a dark corridor—as part of the suspense or the dread, you can gaze into that darkness, you can cut to the anxious face of the explorer, you can have the camera itself edge into the dark space. It is just like the question mark in storytelling itself. The parent guides and teases the child at the same time—"and then . . . and then . . . and? . . ." But the parent wants to end the story. Dinner is waiting, and the child needs to sleep. We do not like to attach terror to the process of sleep. So the suspense must end tidily and with warmth: " . . . and do you know what was hiding at the end of the corridor? . . . It was a little kitten, or a doll. . . . And here's the doll: it's yours."

In the cinema, the manipulation of suspense is one of the prime instruments of storytelling. But we all fear that the lovely calm of questioning will give way to the babble of explaining. And some viewers get out at that point, just as they throw away an Agatha Christie novel when Poirot goes into his owlish account of his own cleverness.

Psycho is a course in menacing suspense. It is a roller-coaster ride in which the gradual tightening tension of the first forty minutes needs to explode—though the shower sunburst is still a great surprise. The film then regathers itself. It has that long, nearly silent cleanup operation in which the slower rhythms of reordering say to us, "Don't worry, I won't do that to you again, at least not yet." The second climax is the death of Arbogast, and it's pretty and rueful enough in one way—for the inquirer is extinguished—but the manner of the crane shot is so hysterically ingenious that it stinks of fabrication. Showing off is being used to mask a lack of content. The film has run out of mystery, and it now hangs on the downhill run toward the "answer," the payoff. Hitchcock has lost interest, and he has known all along that his payoff in *Psycho* is a drab concession to the trashiness of "slasher" horror movies. He is about to betray the fascinating Norman he offered in the supper scene.

More profoundly, he risks betraying fascination itself, for in a mystery film nothing is as seductive as not knowing. An explanation beggars the whole game. There is nothing that mystery dreads more than the banality of explanation or coming clean. Consider, by contrast, John Boorman's film *Point Blank*, made in 1967. A man, Walker

(Lee Marvin), is betrayed on the abandoned island of Alcatraz after a robbery and seemingly left for dead. But he comes back from the dead, like a sleepwalker, and makes his way through the members of the syndicate in search of his mythic $93,000. We are not sure whether he is dead and dreaming or really alive again. Is he man or myth? The lovely air of that question guards him artistically, until the end when he is apparently face-to-face with the packet of money he has pursued. At which point, Walker vanishes. He does not come forward for his prize. Does he withdraw in fear of more conspiracy? Has the dreamer died? The film is saved by a concluding note of fresh mystery.

In several other films—in *Rear Window*, in *Vertigo*, in *North by Northwest*, say—Hitchcock remains gripping to the last shot because he keeps the human drama unfolding. The great difficulty facing *Psycho* is that our identifier in the film (Janet Leigh) is gone. The only real replacement is Norman Bates—and that isn't going to work. So what would you do? Is there a way of saving *Psycho*'s mystery and its uncanny control?

Fifty years later or so, I suppose you could have the sheriff, Sam, and Lila coming out of church in Fairvale and notice a newcomer and let the movie just slide away with that newcomer's story. That's how *Psycho* had worked once, with Marion's story slipping into Norman's. What is the third story? I don't know—perhaps it's the girl in the hardware store who realizes that Sam has been tricking her, and so she picks up straightaway with another man, a traveling salesman passing through town, a man who has a wife in many small towns in northern California as he pushes his trade selling gardening tools.

You know and I know that instead of that radical second departure from normalcy, any thorough account of *Psycho* is going to have to go through the scenes—rich in specious clues—where Lila goes into the house, explores the mother's room and Norman's room, retreats down into the fruit cellar, finds the corpse of Mrs. Bates, and so on. If I say this stuff stinks, I mean not just amateur taxidermy—it's simply not worthy of the first half of *Psycho*. Not even when the wig knocked off Norman's head seems to seethe and live in the swaying light. I mean that it's impossible that the mother's corpse sits up as a living person. Above all, I mean that I don't credit half a second of this rigmarole about Mother having taken over Norman.

And as is often the case, the emotional truth of it all has been discarded or omitted. Remember, if I ask you, "Who killed Mrs. Bates?" the answer is "Norman." He killed his mother and her lover once he had seen that they meant more to each other than the son meant to the mother. So Norman is the killer—in which case Mother has a grievance and a need for vengeance. This needs a lot of rewriting. Suppose the new inquiring figure is not Lila but Marion's mother, revealed as a possessive, anxiety-ridden woman who helps us see how much she has smothered her daughter. And it needs a Norman—a play actor more than a psycho—who takes delight in retreating into the role of his mother so that he can lose the guilt he feels toward her. Here is an emotional story that might make the whole crazed film coherent. It's the Norman already created at the end—in the coda, that sudden return to greatness—where the hunched son watches the camera but speaks as the mother. I'm suggesting Marion's mother for two reasons: Hitch was fascinated with mothers, and Marion's mother talking to Norman (it is an immense feat of writing) could be a scene to match the supper scene. But suppose Marion's mother is played by Marion, or suppose the demented Mrs. Bates sees a harrowed, bloodied Marion come back from the shower.

Are you nervous about these speculations? There's no need to be. This recasting of the story line is one of the things scriptwriters do—I'm sure it's the kind of thing Stefano and Hitchcock tried as they prepared the picture.

Whole excursions of narrative may be proposed and written—only to be discarded.

"YOU NEED SOMEONE TO EXPLAIN IT ALL"

As they worked on the script, Joe Stefano suggested to Hitchcock that too much had been jammed into the last minutes of suspense and action: so Mrs. Bates is a rotting corpse, and "Mother" is Norman in a fright wig. But why? What has happened to Norman's mind? Hitch was nervous. He said he thought too solemn an explanation might be boring—and even unbelievable. And Stefano actually recommended the big, bluff, garrulous Simon Oakland to play the psychiatrist.

After the scene with the psychiatrist had been shot, Hitchcock is reported to have put his arm around Oakland and thanked him for saving the picture. I suppose what he meant was that Oakland—like all the supports in the film—had done a good, persuasive job in a way that stopped the audience from laughing out loud at fanciful material. But what needed to be "saved" was the film's and Hitchcock's indifference to the stated content. I don't think he ever believed in this idea of a character taking over another—only in the ways it could be filmed. Yet the fact remains, in scenario terms, that once you've chosen to go that way, you're bound to deal with it, or tidy it up.

Oakland's character (speaking in front of a map of Shasta County) does the second cleanup job. He lets us go home with the sweet dream that this ghastly act has been dealt with. There is an explanation, and there is even the final Norman/Mother scene to go with it. It's nowhere near enough, just as Perkins's Norman seems a more sophisticated boy than the real Bates could ever have been. Perkins flirts with the idea of a gay Norman, and that plays into the scheme of him as a frenzied actor, always putting on a different persona. That's how he wears "Mother" and that's the quiet, deadly brilliance of the last scene where Norman and Mother's voice speaks to us in that chilling direct stare—it is as if Norman has always known we would be intimate. And, of course, it ends in the coup of his looking up under his eyebrows, dissolving through the skull of his mother to a view of the car, the white car, being pulled up out of the shit. Marion will be inside, still quite fresh, with the money as good as new. And in that last meticulously controlled

optical, the skull itself seems to grin and Hitchcock himself seems to stare through the fussy lace curtaining of
"psychological explanation" with what is the real point
of the picture: that his pulling our leg took priority over
our minds.

   Gotcha!

5

Hitch-Cock

PSYCHO OPENED IN 1960, in mid-June, and it's inter-esting to consider the tonal gap between it and the other American films that opened in that year: *Let's Make Love* (one of the last complete films from Marilyn Monroe); Otto Preminger's *Exodus*; *Wild River* by Elia Kazan; *The Apartment* by Billy Wilder; Burt Lancaster in *Elmer Gantry*; *The Magnificent Seven*; *Spartacus*; Jerry Lewis as *The Bellboy*; the British film *Sons and Lovers*; Olivier in *The Entertainer*; John Wayne's *The Alamo*. Of course, that moment, 1959–1960, is the breaking of the French New Wave. By contrast with that, so many American films seemed set in old ways. There were just two pictures from America in 1960 that were radical, dangerous (to the system, at least), and quite new as experiences—*Psycho* and John Cassavetes' *Shadows*.

There had been an odd warning of the risks in *Psycho*. One of Hitch's contemporaries in British film was Michael Powell. They were not quite friends, but far from enemies, and they were both of them touched by genius. It happened that in March 1960, three months before the opening of *Psycho*, Powell had opened his brave departure film, *Peeping Tom*. It was as nasty as *Psycho* and touched with the same kind of black humor. It was about a young filmmaker who murders women (using a leg of his camera tripod as a sword stick) while filming them to capture the look of terror. The film was so trashed by the critics—on the grounds of its cynical bad taste and its playing with sadism—that Powell's career was halted for years. The director of *A Matter of Life and Death*, *Black Narcissus*, and *The Red Shoes* was at a standstill. Hitch only had to be afraid of fear to have premonitions about *Psycho*.

Making *Psycho* was one part of its genius. Opening it with aplomb was the other. In postproduction he fought brilliant battles with the censors, until they were lost in the film's details and prepared to let it pass. There were previews at which close associates believed the film was either a sensation or ridiculous, but they could not decide which.

But Hitch had his last weapon to come—the score by Bernard Herrmann. Just as in the past, Herrmann had made a musical story that lifted *Citizen Kane* and *Vertigo*, and just as he would yet again later, with *Taxi Diver*, so the music carried a picture past realism and into mythology. Very often in his career Hitch and his screenwriters ended up at odds, envious of each other's creative contributions. It was a nasty habit in the director, but he knew enough— for the moment—not to sever ties with Herrmann. It is in the music that *Psycho* reaches out for the fusion of film and opera, the most fruitful future direction for the art and maybe the business. Time and again, it is the music that turns doubt about seriousness into majestic effect.

One of the editors on the film, Terry Williams, recalled the day the first score was laid in as a track. Like archaeologists retrieving shards of bone, the editors had pored over the details of slaughter and lost sight of it. With the music, suddenly they were screaming as if the film were new.

Paramount executives were still not comfortable with the picture, but they pushed for their way of releasing it until Lew Wasserman had to remind them that Hitch was the majority owner of the venture. Indeed, this was very rare: as the 60 percent proprietor, he did not have to bow to the studio in cutting the picture or in adjusting the advertising. It is often said that Orson Welles enjoyed the most generous contract ever in Hollywood, with *Citizen Kane*, in that, providing he stayed on budget, he had freedom of script, casting, and cut. But Hitchcock had all those rights, and when the picture made money he had 60 percent of the profits, a detail Welles had never bothered with—as if he hardly anticipated profits.

It was Wasserman who advised big featured openings in Los Angeles and New York, to be followed by the widest possible release quickly. This was an unusual approach. In those days, release patterns were far more gradual than is true now. Interest in a movie was allowed to build slowly, and tastefully. But Wasserman believed it was a vulgar business, so why not get as many people as possible in a state of wanting to see a movie now? He fought that battle over the years and is generally regarded as having finally won it with the summer opening of *Jaws*—a Hitchcockian suspense film—in 400 theaters simultaneously. Of course, today that number is well over 3,000 screens for the big pictures. This has several consequences: most films make their money (or they don't) far quicker than once upon a time, and in the first-weekend frenzy (suitably stoked by television advertising) the critical doubts are more easily overlooked. Yes, there were some fears that critics would attack *Psycho*, but the answer was to preempt such considerations with a blanket opening policy.

The other coup was the trailer. Hitchcock was by then widely known for the poker-faced intros to his television show. So he employed the same method on a rather grander scale for his new movie. Now he was a kind of realtor showing off the Bates Motel for prospective buyers. So he was dry and dusty, and then struck by how much it had all been tidied up since—since the blood, and then for an instant you were into the shower mayhem and that crude but very effective dare that still gets people to the movies: "Can you stand to see this?" The trailer was inspired and characteristic, and it was a fair warning: for this new story was itself a mockery of story, advertising, and the whole apparatus of "coming attractions." It was going to cut the blonde to pieces while pulling our leg, and the hint was in—that slaughter wasn't really serious. The meaning of the film was always compromised by its commercial nature.

The next step was to enforce a policy that Hitch had attempted on *Vertigo*, but which lapsed there simply because the film was not compelling enough. Thus, the edict went out in advance that no one would be let in to see *Psycho*

once the film had started. The reason given for this was
that the story had such twists, the customer would be
cheating himself if he got the ending before the beginning.

This was directly against common cinematic practice.
Films were shown continually, and many people came in
during the picture and then left when the story became familiar again. I know that sounds awful, yet the condition
prevailed—and now there were life-size cardboard-cutout
figures of Hitchcock himself in theater lobbies, wagging a
finger and insisting that no one, positively no one, would
be let in once the film had started. Of course, a weird underlying frisson attached to that severity—that you might
not be allowed out of the dark, either, if the fear proved unbearable. Audiences were tickled, stirred, and amused—
and that balance did accurately reflect the nature of *Psycho*.
The tongue-in-cheek trailer was a signal of a devastating
movie yet one with a strange, sardonic flourish. The advertising was intimidating, but it carried a new respect for
movies and those who made them.

The reviews never made much difference because of the
fantastic launch that the film received. The suggestion of
an uncommon flirtation with violence in a front-rank film
worked. The trailer and the tight security over admissions
inflamed word of mouth. And people who saw the film

early were shattered by it. I saw it myself at the Plaza in London in the first days of its run. I was there for the midday show, and I recall seeing it with very few people in the theater. But that wasn't bad. Somehow the solitude added to the intensity. Even at nineteen, it was a very scary experience. Once the terrible or unthinkable thing had happened—the slaughter of Marion—one was begging for nothing else as devastating. One didn't rationalize this straightaway, but the message emerged: no screen murder had ever been shot with such care, invention, or "perfection." So when Lila entered the Bates house and made her way to the fruit cellar, I was not yet in command of my lofty theory that the second half of the film is a concoction. The tension worked, as did the cutting from tracking shots forward from Lila's point of view to shots backing off in front of her where she seems to urge the camera forward. People are brave in Hitchcock because of his remorseless command of space.

I was a directed viewer at the Plaza in 1960. I dare say that worked for most of the early viewers, and I know that I was desperate to get friends to see *Psycho* immediately. Indeed, I had only lately started film school, where I found myself posed against the social realist tendencies of the teaching staff. I was certain that *Psycho* was the film of the year and essential material for film students, whereas the respectable film according to my teachers—it had been produced by the man who headed the film school—was Guy Green's *The Angry Silence*, a story of union troubles in British industry. This comparison seems fatuous now, but this really was the current argument.

The range of opinions on *Psycho* was fascinating. In the *New York Times*, Bosley Crowther's opinion built through the summer. At first he had found the film crude and old-fashioned. But he looked again and thought it "fascinating" and "provocative." By the end of the year, he rated it one of the year's ten best. This was despite a running argument in the paper's letters to the editor where *Psycho* was often called "morbid" and "sickening." In *Esquire*, Dwight Macdonald said it came from "a mean, sly, sadistic little mind." *Time* said it was just a "creak-and-shriek movie." In London, in *Sight and Sound*, the magazine's editor, Penelope Houston, went to the length of calling it a minor, unimportant film, though unfortunately characteristic of the new French attitude to film. And in an unlikely place, Oxford, a student, V. F. Perkins, wrote, "The first time it is only a splendid entertainment, a 'very minor film.' But when one can no longer be distracted from the characters by an irrelevant 'mystery,' *Psycho* becomes immeasurably rewarding as well as much more thrilling."

All of which was a portent of things to come. But, still, *Psycho* made its own rules and was regarded as a cunning but nasty exploitation film. That is the only way of reading the best-director nomination for Hitchcock, while the film was ignored. Today, that split is exposed as a travesty. The Academy looks foolish, but so do we—because we were apparently incapable of admitting to, let alone explaining, the true film sensation of the year. It would gross something like $15 million in its first release, and that meant eventual earnings of at least $4 million to Hitchcock himself. It was a lot more successful than his recent hits: *Rear Window* grossed $5.7 million, *North by Northwest* $6 million, *To Catch a Thief* $4.5 million, and *The Man Who Knew Too Much* $4.1 million.

Psycho had helped make Hitchcock one of the most consistently successful picture makers in America of the last decade—if you liked gruesome thrills. The fact that *Psycho* was not nominated that year by the Academy is shocking. The five candidates for Best Picture would be *The Apartment, The Alamo, Elmer Gantry, Sons and Lovers*, and *The Sundowners* (today, it's hard to believe the last four were rated ahead of *Psycho*). *The Apartment*, by

Billy Wilder, would win the Oscar, and it grossed $6.7 million. It was regarded as a smart, sour comedy and a portrait of modern America. Yet its appetite for nastiness is not too far from the tone of Hitchcock's film.

Hitch got his fifth nomination as best director—along with Wilder, Jack Cardiff for *Sons and Lovers*, Jules Dassin for *Never on Sunday*, and Fred Zinnemann for *The Sundowners*. It was Wilder's second win and sixth nomination. And *The Apartment* is a good picture, witty, intelligent, pessimistic. It may have been the film that fitted in best with what America reckoned it should think of itself at the time.

Anthony Perkins was not nominated! Could nobody in the movie establishment read his startling balance of camp and pathos? Janet Leigh got a nod for best supporting actress (the award went to Shirley Jones in *Elmer Gantry*). There was no nomination for screenplay, nor for editing. There was no nomination for Bernard Herrmann's score, one of the most decisive in the history of film—the prize went to Ernest Gold for his score for *Exodus*. Instead, there were nominations to Joseph Hurley, Robert Clatworthy, and George Milo for black-and-white art direction. That seemed like a limp joke in that the decor had been treated with strategic disrespect throughout the project. John L. Russell was nominated for cinematography. In hindsight, that is achingly deserved. Russell changed the way we look at things in *Psycho*. You can say he did his master's bidding—his master would have said that. But whereas the photography on *The Apartment* is effective, the look of *Psycho* is a new acid-rural poetry and a medium that was plainly under threat. So there are a few black-and-white pictures that are not just beautiful but warnings to a careless age—*Psycho*, *Raging Bull*, Antonioni's *La Notte*. But *Psycho* was the only one that had had a television cameraman.

The Academy Awards aside, Hitchcock was in triumph. In the spring of 1961, in Paris, he was feted, not just by critics and cineasts but by wine enthusiasts. He was given a great honor—that of *tastevin*—and the claims for his genius at film mounted. Clearly, in addition, Hitchcock was thrilled to see that his young followers had become filmmakers themselves. And although the intense and self-preoccupied theorizing of *Cahiers* had stayed a largely French matter through the '50s, it was now breaking on foreign shores. In Britain, there was an eager controversy going on over the nature of film itself in which Hitchcock and *Psycho* were employed by both sides as ammunition. And in America it was becoming apparent that a new young generation was taking film and writing about it very seriously. There were signs that film might even penetrate the walls of academe. And to the extent that Hitchcock made films that were like theory in demonstration, he was an ideal figure in teaching as well as a new example of the "auteur." *Psycho* was a test case in the debate as to whether "crass" commercial films could be art.

At another level, it was clear that the maneuvers over *Psycho* between Paramount and Universal had determined Hitchcock's commercial future. Since he had benefited so much from the deal done by Lew Wasserman, there was little doubt about which way he would go. He was given a building of his own at Universal, the biggest of the studio bungalows. It included offices for his storyboarding work, editing rooms, a kitchen, a cocktail lounge, and a private dining room. It was the world according to Norman Bates, but on an unimaginable scale of luxury and prestige. Naturally enough, Wasserman and Universal wondered what he would do next.

HITCHCOCK USUALLY HAD a gang of projects, in his head or on his bookshelf. He toyed with the idea of a blind jazz pianist who solves crimes. He had noticed a short story by

Daphne Du Maurier, "The Birds." But he was most interested in a novel by Winston Graham, *Marnie*, about a woman who is a chronic thief and whose husband takes her cure in hand. He also liked that project because Grace Kelly, or Princess Grace of Monaco, liked it. In the spring of 1961, Hitch met every day with Joseph Stefano to make a treatment from the Graham novel that was sent to Grace Kelly. We don't know what was happening in Monaco, but it seems clear that Kelly herself wanted to go back to work and believed it would be possible. If only from wishful thinking, Hitch clung to this hope, and as he worked on *Marnie* he saw Kelly in the role of the tortured young woman who has to balance respectability and a need to steal things that is directly aligned with her sexual frigidity. But then word came from Monaco that Kelly could not possibly film *Marnie* in 1962. There were prior engagements. Would Hitch wait a year? There was no doubt that he would: Kelly's return would have been a commercial coup, but it was also a chance to grill the greatest of his screen loves.

In "The Birds," first published in 1952, a remote farming community in England is overtaken by an invasion of birds. The characters in the story are not well delineated or given any depth. Rather, the story is a fable, perched on the edge of science fiction and ruminations about the end of the world. "I only read the story once," Hitch would say later. "I couldn't tell you what it was about today." But he had been reminded of the story in the early '60s by reports—from California—of unusual bird behavior and what might be interpreted as attacks.

Hitchcock looked for a writer. He tried novelist James Kennaway but was terribly put off when Kennaway had a brainstorm—of doing the film without showing a single bird. Clearly, Hitch was committed to a full treatment of the birds—it was why he was doing the picture. He considered Wendell Mayes and Ray Bradbury before falling in with Evan Hunter, a novelist, screenwriter, and the creator of the Ed McBain thrillers. In the second half of 1961, in close cooperation and good spirits, the two men wrote *The Birds* for the screen—and as a complete departure from the Du Maurier story.

Their script reflects on *Psycho* in fascinating ways. Melanie Daniels is a madcap heiress and a very unhappy young woman. She has broken ties with her parents. One day in a pet shop in San Francisco, she meets Mitch Brenner and his young sister, Cathy. Melanie and Mitch flirt, and she decides later to buy a pair of lovebirds for the younger sister and deliver them personally to the Brenner home in Bodega Bay, about an hour north of San Francisco.

Having made that journey, she discovers that Mitch and his sister live with their mother, Lydia, an emotionally controlling person. Lydia is hostile to Melanie. But anyone can see that Mitch and Melanie are falling in love—further, anyone can see that Lydia and Melanie look alike (it is a resemblance played upon without ever being fully defined, like the pairing of Sam and Norman in *Psycho*). As this interplay proceeds, so the birds make small forays against people in Bodega Bay, until their larger campaign is clear. The birds attack. Melanie breaks down after suffering an immense ordeal and almost total attack on her personally by the birds. Mitch drives the family away, but the birds are left in charge of the world.

Melanie hardly knew her own mother. She has been as neglected as Mitch has been watchdogged by his mother. The Brenner house is to the north of the city, and it is in the upstairs of the house that the greatest threat will be found. It is late in the film that Melanie hears a noise in the besieged house and goes upstairs—rather as Lila dares to explore the Bates house in *Psycho*. What she finds is an attic full of waiting birds—and they descend on her. The actress who played Melanie had a week of shooting in which she was the object of pecking, thrusting, swooping birds, and in which she was nearly catatonic. That bird assault is akin to the shower savagery.

Who would play Melanie? In conversation with Evan Hunter, Hitch had smiled and said, "Well, of course, Grace would have been perfect" — smart, classy, teasing, brittle, and then breaking. He looked at footage of several young actresses — Pamela Franklin, Sandra Dee, Carol Lynley, Yvette Mimieux. And in the hunt he saw some footage of a fashion model named Tippi Hedren. She was thirty, of Swedish descent, but born in Minnesota. She was ash blonde, unusually pale, beautiful, but with a faint streak of potential victim. She wore clothes perfectly and moved very well. She was a divorced mother, and she had a daughter of her own named Melanie (that child would become Melanie Griffith, the actress).

Hitchcock put her under personal contract at five hundred dollars a week. He had a couple of other actresses under personal contract, but not much happened with their careers. He talked to Hedren and gave her advice on clothes and her looks. He even asked her to screen a lot of his old films, and he prepared a kind of anthology of great scenes with actresses in his work. Then he called for a screen test.

With Robert Burks, Hitch's regular cameraman, doing the photography, and with Martin Balsam (Arbogast) standing in as all the men in the scenes, Tippi passed the test as an ideal actress for Hitchcock. At Chasen's restaurant, in Los Angeles, a few nights later, with his wife, Alma, and Lew Wasserman present, he gave Hedren a brooch featuring birds in flight and said the part was hers.

The Birds began shooting in the early spring of 1962, with Hedren and her costars, Rod Taylor (as Mitch) and Jessica Tandy (as Lydia). It saw Hitchcock revert to his standard crew: cameraman Robert Burks, art director Robert Boyle, editor George Tomasini, and Bernard Herrmann again as composer. In addition, he had hired veteran animator Ub Iwerks to do some of the trick-shot animation of the birds. At about the same time, François Truffaut was dining in New York with Bosley Crowther, film critic of the *New York Times*, and Herman G. Weinberg, head of film at the Museum of Modern Art. He was startled at their low estimate of Hitch and realized once again how the British director was a test case. He wondered what to do that might raise Hitchcock's reputation—and his own, too.

On June 2, 1962, he wrote a personal letter to Hitchcock, reminding the great man of their previous meetings and of the "propaganda" work carried out on Hitch's behalf by *Cahiers du Cinema*. What Truffaut now proposed was a book, for as Truffaut had himself become a director, so his admiration for Hitch had grown: "There are many directors with a love for the cinema, but what you possess is a love of celluloid itself and it is that which I would like to talk to you about." Truffaut proposed a book based on interviews—perhaps eight days' solid work—to cover all of Hitchcock's career. "If the idea were to appeal to you, and you agreed to do it, here is how I think we might proceed: I could come and stay for about ten days wherever it would be most convenient for you. From New York I would bring with me Miss Helen Scott who would be the ideal interpreter; she carries out simultaneous translations at such a speed that we would have the impression of speaking to one another without any intermediary and, working as she does at the French Film Office in New York, she is also completely familiar with the vocabulary of the cinema. She and I take rooms in the hotel closest to your home or whichever office you might arrange."

The letter reached Hitchcock while he was still shooting *The Birds*. But he cabled back immediately: "Dear Monsieur Truffaut. Your letter brought tears to my eyes and I am so grateful to receive such a tribute from you. I am still shooting *The Birds* and this will continue until 15 July and after that I will have to begin editing which will take me several weeks. I think I will wait until we have finished shooting *The Birds* and then I will contact you with the idea of getting together around the end of August. Thank you again for your charming letter."

Alfred Hitchcock's formal education ended when he was only thirteen. His self-education in film, or celluloid, and storytelling never stopped. But he was a working-class boy impressed by learning all the more because he had had so little. The invitation from Truffaut must have seemed overwhelming and rewarding. I doubt that the reference to tears is mere politeness. Here was a moment at which a significant part of the outer world had stepped forward to substantiate Hitchcock's self-esteem and his view of movies. He was valuable. He might be a genius. In Britain and America, his world, that label had hardly been used before, except perhaps for Chaplin.

More or less, this letter came to him as he was shooting the most intense week of *The Birds*, the week that had been set aside on a special set to cover the ordeal of Melanie and the ultimate bird attack (the equivalent of the shower murder in *Psycho*—shot as lovingly as a romantic scene). This time there was no fear of nudity or "personal violence." But Tippi Hedren had assumed the birds would be fake. Hitch said no, they were going to have to use real creatures. "Another special set had been built for the scene, surrounded by a huge cage to keep the birds from soaring into the rafters. Inside the cage were a crew of propmen, wearing thick leather gloves to their elbows to protect themselves. Although the gulls were trained, they quickly learned to avoid Hedren, and had to be hurled at her by the propmen. Air jets kept the birds from flying into the camera lens. This extraordinary scene, which occupies roughly one minute of screen time, took an entire week to shoot, and it became a grueling physical ordeal—but especially for the leading lady."

By the end of the week, Hedren was cracking. She had been pecked near her eye. Hitchcock was so distressed that he kept to his office while they were preparing. But he was there for every shot. And somehow or other, in the crisis, he seemed able to justify what he was doing because he was Hitchcock, and because he was falling in love with the actress and the power he held over her. In the end, what *Psycho* had been about was a strange kind of permission that comes with voyeurism—if you let me see you, then I can destroy you, or spare you.

Imagine this *Psycho:* Marion is in the shower. Norman arrives, with his frenzy of stabbing motions. But she is not touched, let alone pierced. The whole thing is like a mating ritual. But she faints, and when she wakes up, there she is, in Mother's bed, with Norman watching her and smiling. Because he has won her.

TRUFFAUT'S BOOK was agreed upon. Éditions Robert Laffont would publish it in France and Simon and Schuster in New York. In August 1962 Truffaut and Helen Scott arrived in Los Angeles. They stayed at the Beverly Hills Hotel and spent the next days working with Hitchcock in his offices on the Universal lot. It was a detailed conversation about a working life, and later chapters would be added to cover both *The Birds* and *Marnie*. In addition, Truffaut went to the National Film Archive in London to get frame illustrations so that key sequences (like the shower scene) could be done as autopsies. The book was published in Paris in 1966 and in New York a year later.

That publication process was so slow that another shorter interview reached print first: that was conducted by Peter Bogdanovich in 1963 for the Museum of Modern Art.

Its reach was far less, and it lacked the lavish illustration of the book. But there could be no doubt: Hitchcock had become a subject in American culture.

In which case, we have to marvel at the ugliness of the way Hitchcock now sought to impose himself on his world. *The Birds* was not nearly the success that *Psycho* had been, but people were amazed by how this aging director had used new effects (of picture and sound) to sharpen the malice of the birds. The screenwriter, Evan Hunter, who had witnessed Hitch's indifference to what the birds might mean firsthand, was now amused, yet distressed, by the way the director was available for any and every parable of significance. Hunter had known that Hitch had no other aim except to frighten the audience. But the subject of earnest interviews needed more weight. And so *The Birds*—which was in postproduction during the Cuban missile crisis of October 1962—became a story about the end of the world and man's complacency. In truth, of course, it was a strange sadomasochistic transference between actress and director.

Briefly, the old song was sung—that Grace Kelly might return for *Marnie*—but it was not clear now that Hitchcock wanted her. Nor should anyone diminish the quality of Tippi Hedren just because the director had become obsessed with her. The heroine has a wan, invalid-like personality in both films, and it comes from the relative insubordination of Hedren. She was trying so hard to do what Hitchcock wanted, and then she was late in the day in appreciating that she was fulfilling his sick fantasy. When he admitted his feelings, she was horrified. There was no chance of his dream coming true. But she could also see how vulnerable this hitherto masked man had become in letting his true feelings show so much. He was humiliated; he was old and utterly unsuited to a romantic role. But the power of film had carried him away, and he had thought that miracles—like Grace becoming a real princess—might be repeated. Hedren is touching in *Marnie*, but its looming rape sequence (which horrified Evan Hunter and finally drove him from the picture) is all too palpably significant. Hunter said that it was a scene that preoccupied Hitch to an unhealthy degree. Once upon a time, the voyeur had had an expert, mischievous, self-controlling restraint. But with *Psycho* he had started to indulge it, and now in *Marnie* it began to look like prurience. What's more, Hedren accused Hitchcock of enforcing her contract (five hundred dollars a week) for another two years without giving her anything to do.

It is hardly clear what Hitchcock intended. Would he have settled for mere sex with Hedren? Or did he plan to discard his wife, Alma, and readjust his entire life—to match the fantasy lives of the great Hollywood moguls?

6

Other Bodies in the Swamp

THE EXTENDED SIGNIFICANCE of "the moment of *Psycho*" is not just the impact of an isolated sensation but the spreading influence it exerted on other films, especially in the treatment of sex and violence, and the room it opened up for the ironic (or mocking) treatment of both. Thus, "My mother's not herself today" is a taster for so many Clint Eastwood lines, like, "Do you feel lucky? Well, do you, punk?" Such lines encouraged our habit of talking back to the screen and making a game out of death.

The list that follows is not exhaustive. It does not include every remake of Hitchcock material, and it passes over the forlorn sequels to *Psycho* itself where a rare actor, Anthony Perkins, was squeezed dry. Still, the desperation in those films was a telling commentary on invention in the 1980s and '90s and how *psycho* had gone from being a warning to a term of caustic endearment.

PSYCHO'S FILM LEGACY

Films are not intended as a stepping-stone path, but so many new films follow a direction and an energy that have worked in the past. *Psycho* uncovered new clues about that journey: that we did not care too much about the "nice" people, the ones we liked; that we were determined not to be surprised by blood and its flow—we know these things will come; and that we are mesmerized by some of the people who do damage. It is as if the medium itself— sitting in the dark and looking at the shining light—was meant to teach us that. The new tone in cinema said, "Believe less in the story and its characters, but study the game being played."

1962: *Dr. No* and the Bond Franchise

The first of the Ian Fleming 007 books was published in 1953; it took several years and a substantial reappraisal of the material to make those taut but inert novels work on-screen. The immense franchise would depend on tongue-in-cheek attitudes toward sex and violence and toward the superhero himself, a descendant of the Richard Hannay figure Hitch had once enjoyed in *The 39 Steps* (1935). That comic edge was created for the films to make Bond's brutal opportunism more palatable. The films were full of double entendres that helped soften or excuse the sadism and the erotic objectification of women. It's clear in hindsight that Hitchcock was a point of reference in the discovery of a tone that would let the audience laugh at things that were once beyond laughter, because of cruelty or sexual exploitation. Even if Hitch had not cast Sean Connery as one of his heroes (Mark Rutland, the husband in *Marnie*), the linkage is inescapable.

1962: *What Ever Happened to Baby Jane?*

Robert Aldrich's gruesome mockery of a Hollywood ghost story was an important addition of macabre comedy to the horror genre, as well as a further play on the new "gotcha"—that old ladies can be frightening and dangerous. You can feel the picture enlisting the cruel energies of the audience and hurling them at the stricken characters. As for the grand old movie stars Bette Davis and Joan

Crawford, the business could do whatever it chose to them after the unexpected dispatch of Janet Leigh.

1962: *Lolita*

Hitchcock and Nabokov were correspondents who actually thought of working together. But *Lolita* is a love story in which the reader/viewer is often enlisted on the side of the villain's wordplay and pointed point of view. The shocking sexual content of the material had a great deal to do with the comic erudition of that voice. Moreover, James Mason's Humbert is very little removed from his suave Vandamm in *North by Northwest*, another crazy chase film in which the pursuit will redefine the love story. Nabokov sometimes praised himself for the cleanliness of his sexual narrative, just as Hitch led the applause for the lack of flesh piercing in the shower sequence.

1962: *The Manchurian Candidate*

It's true that Hitchcock seldom took politics seriously, but the complex setup in the first half of *Candidate* is not unlike Hitchcock's shift from one picture to another in the middle of *Psycho*. Moreover, the scheme of deranged heroes and richly portrayed villains is also in the Hitchcock tradition. Angela Lansbury is not just the mother a son is going to have to shoot; she is confirmation that the milk of American motherhood has turned sour. When her Mrs. Iselin kisses zombie son Raymond (Laurence Harvey) on the mouth, we know that some mothers grip their numb sons by their gonads.

1963: *The Nutty Professor*

Jerry Lewis's film is a grab bag for many American dreams and nightmares. Its use of the Jekyll and Hyde motif is encouraged by the dainty ways in which Norman Bates can step over his own line. Lewis was owning up to enormous hostilities within the American dream and the sudden way in which a goofy nerd could become a rat with teeth. The paradox in Lewis would last decades: drumming up money for damaged children while playing one for laughs.

1965: *The Collector*

This film comes from a best-selling novel by John Fowles, but the situation of the lovely young woman held prisoner by a disturbed youth is too close to *Psycho* to be casual. Equally, the setup of *The Collector* is a story that plays into our mounting habit of voyeurism. Do we want the girl to escape, or is the setup begging for her submission?

1965: *Repulsion*

Roman Polanski is one of those filmmakers most fond of and affected by Hitchcock. His film *Repulsion* is a clever replay of the lovely blonde under duress who turns nasty as she breaks down. Moreover, her anger burns exactly those cruel upper-class Brits that Hitch liked to abuse. Polanski is obsessed with prison as a condition—and his world reminds us of the traps that Marion and Norman discuss together. In Polanski, the walls have limbs and lungs, but the kitchen is the most dangerous place. Moreover, the idea of total blind panic (like repulsion) is at the heart of *Psycho*'s analysis of Norman. Neither director really believes in common sense—but perhaps the movies prefer life that way.

1966: *Blow-Up*

Here is an elegant existential mystery that casually uncovers pubic hair. As such, it was a landmark in the steady retreat of the tide of censorship. You can see that breakdown in hundreds of films, but *Blow-Up* is intriguing because most of its coups have a funny side. But, of course, finally, Antonioni had made one of the great voyeuristic traps, and no one so bent on watching can work without Hitchcock looking over his shoulder.

1967: *Bonnie and Clyde*

Warren Beatty and Arthur Penn had little thought of following in Hitchcock's steps. But the script for this film, and the violent association of comedy and murder, was originally intended for François Truffaut after the impact of films like *Tirez sur le pianiste*. What alarmed viewers of *Bonnie and Clyde* was the good time they were having (or being allowed to have) with violence. There was a public outcry, but the onset of violence made the censorship anxieties of *Psycho* look ancient. In fifty years, our capacity for seeing pain has increased beyond all reason. Does that mean we have become more cruel, or more voyeuristic?

1969: *Le Boucher*

Remember Chabrol, coauthor of that first book on Hitch-cock in 1957? No one has made more films so subtly in-fluenced by the themes and situations in Hitchcock as Chabrol, and if I select *Le Boucher* here for observation, it is not to rule out many others worth consideration. Stéphane Audran is a schoolteacher living in the Dor-dogne. She is nearly perfect, but she is cold. There is a killer loose in the savage natural beauty of that part of France. We suspect the butcher (Jean Yanne). He in turn adores Audran but cannot reach her except through the living myth of being a great murderer. This is an extraordi-nary character study and an analysis of what murder can mean in sterile lives. The two actors play as if in a trance. The "beauty" of the world drifts by like a great lost ship. The small tremor of terrible violence, of murder, knits the film, and all the sex and violence are repressed—a testa-ment to how thoroughly Chabrol grasped Hitchcock.

1969: *Mississippi Mermaid*

How could Truffaut not have his Hitchcock period, influ-enced by the book they had done together? People point to *The Bride Wore Black* as its apotheosis, but I find that film intellectually forced. The real Hitch film by Truffaut is *Mississippi Mermaid*, in which a wealthy tobacco farmer (Jean-Paul Belmondo) on the island of Reunion receives his mail-order bride. But she looks not so much like her photograph as she does Catherine Deneuve (always a Hitchcockian blonde). They marry. They seem happy. Then she is gone, with his money. He follows her to France. He tracks her down. She is contrite. She had a terrible life. Truly, she loves him. He relents. It all happens again. Where does rescue join hands with self-destruction? Here is a film that could go on forever.

1971: *A Clockwork Orange*

Kubrick and Hitchcock had a lot of things in common: an extreme appetite for technique that sometimes forgot "content"; a recognition of watching as perhaps the central expression of modern intelligence and a surgeon's interest in the eye; a very cold, sociological gloominess; and a strange confusion of America and Britain that can leave them both looking very unworldly. Alex, in *A Clockwork Orange*, is a psychotic thug who harbors noble aspirations—and, like Norman, he enjoys Beethoven. We find a

record of the Eroica Symphony in Norman's room in the
Bates house, though of course that's also a clue as to the
source of some of the Herrmann music.

1971: *Klute*

A psychological thriller about a woman who needs to
overcome her attraction to self-destruction and a detective
who has a habit of passive watching. The links to *Vertigo*
in Alan Pakula's film are obvious (except that by now the
actress can go naked indefinitely without censorship inter-
vening). Does the evidence proudly borne by Jane Fonda
support the superstition that Janet Leigh also once had
breasts (as opposed to things we could not see)? *Klute* ends
with the killer killed, but there are so many other things to
be afraid of, not least the climate of paranoia.

1972: *Frenzy*

Frenzy is a Hitchcock film, of course, and in some ways
his most disturbing. It is a return to England, to the
Covent Garden produce market where he must have
worked with his father. Glaringly archaic, it is a story
about one man being mistaken for and pursued as a serial

sexual killer. But Hitchcock knows that this is a world in which a film is obliged to show nudity and sexual violence. The killings are set pieces again, but their "candor" is ugly and brutalizing. The old man was making a picture that referred nostalgically to his own past but left people gasping at his nastiness. *Frenzy* is the hardest film to digest for those who want to see Hitch as a great artist instead of a stranded engineer and Englishman.

1973: *Don't Look Now*

This is the Daphne Du Maurier story that Hitchcock did not take up. A married couple, having lost a child through an accidental drowning, go off to Venice in winter. He is helping in the restoration work on an old church. They are trying to recover. But there is a serial killer in Venice, and then the couple start to see a child in a red hooded coat—a figure that reminds them of their lost daughter. This strange horror film, with a half-crazy psychic helping the couple, is loaded with doom. Yet there in the middle it has one of the most uninhibited love scenes ever filmed (Donald Sutherland and Julie Christie). In its warmth and tenderness, and in its solace for two wounded people, it is not just unlike anything in Hitchcock, it is beyond him. Alas,

it all ends badly: the figure in red is a little old lady with a
knife. Let's just say that this sidelong evocation of Hitchcock is a definitive lesson—for him to study.

1974: *The Conversation*

Harry Caul (Gene Hackman) in *The Conversation* is a
Hitchcockian private detective, chronically alone—the
habit of pursuit is not so much his job as his neurotic calling. He is in direct line with Scottie in *Vertigo*, and, like
him, he runs the risk of doing more harm than good. But
there is precise point of reference. As he suspects a murder
has been done in a hotel, Caul discovers—by flushing the
toilet—that all the blood and horror is in the pipes. The
overflowing toilet is a clear reference to *Psycho* as well as
an admission that the censors have all gone home.

1974: *The Texas Chain-Saw Massacre*, et cetera

This must stand for the inexhaustible rural slasher genre
that has done so much to make the American hinterland a
gothic haunted house for paranoids on the road. As the
bloodletting becomes less inhibited, so the domestic cham-
ber of horrors unleashed by the kids whose car breaks

down grows wilder. It leaves us filled with rueful nostalgia for the days when Norman Bates could put an elegant sentence together, and it requires that we regard such dangerous nonsense as "good, clean fun."

1976: *Taxi Driver*

Just over fifteen years after *Psycho*, screen violence had taken over and found tasteful, modern offsetting factors. So when the ratings board found the blood at the end of *Taxi Driver* too flagrant, it was printed less red. After all, it's only a movie. Moreover, the source of the violence, Travis Bickle, goes free. The easy explanation is that film (and its society?) have become so much more sympathetic to the lone-wolf outsider. That has to be not just because we have come to like such people as Norman but because more of us see a glimpse of ourselves in him.

1976: *Obsession*

Scripted by Paul Schrader and directed by Brian De Palma, *Obsession* is a remake of *Vertigo* and a measure of how much the new generation of filmmakers was intent on Hitchcock as a schooling.

1978: *Halloween*

The first in a long series, this low-budget mystery/horror film involves a youth escaped from an asylum and bent on terrible revenge and is essentially aimed at terrorizing pretty young girls. In the 1980s and '90s, such franchises became standard fare. They were called slasher films, and all the long knives came from Mrs. Bates's kitchen drawer (*Halloween* even had a fumbling doctor named Sam Loomis!). Of course, the series coincided with and under-lined the emerging demographic—that filmgoing had become a private playground for sixteen- to twenty-four-year-olds. As the *Scream* films would try to suggest: don't take the terror to heart, because it is only a movie—and the heart is where the knife fits.

1980: *Dressed to Kill*

The most complete homage De Palma would make to Hitchcock and a film with several set pieces worthy of the master himself, such as the intricate pursuit passage where Angie Dickinson thinks she is being flirted with. There is also Miss D in a shower and a bloody murder by a killer dressed in drag. But De Palma worked at his task with the understanding that, by now, there was a large audience that could pick up all the Hitchcock references and accommodate the rather lip-smacking humor in all the physically outraging scenes. It was camp Hitchcock, a summer-vacation *Psycho* for rich kids.

1980: *The Shining*

The Shining comes from a Stephen King novel, but King believed that Kubrick had wasted or missed much of his written terror. That theory held only until King's television remake—a dud. So what stands out now about *The Shining* is a family going back to an unflushed past where the husband has more footing or status than he ever knew. He goes to write his story in the empty Overlook Hotel, but the Overlook is creepy-crawling with stories and characters, like Lloyd the bartender, who are waiting for him, waiting to make old hay again. And if this bad boy Jack may be killed, so what? The house knows that game: it understands precise timetables, and it knows that an elevator shaft is mainlined with blood, walls of blood, breaking in slow motion. But what is really handled is the end of marriage and family. Hitchcock always kept a slight smile on his face, the smile that knows not to trust such groupings.

1986: *Blue Velvet*

The reason to include David Lynch's great film could be sex or violence (it is well supplied with both). But in truth it's his ability to render the screen's flow as a dream—as an unquestionable and immaculate process for which there must be a secret meaning—that most coincides with Hitchcock's momentum. Hitch's steady stress on screen space and celluloid indicates how little interest he had in reality. It's not the road north to Fairvale he follows but a dream trail that is unfolding like back projection behind the sleepwalking sway of Marion's car. It's always the case with Hitchcock that we wait for the spurious details of real places to be lost in the soaring inwardness of dream. So, in *Blue Velvet*, a boy finds an ear and wonders where the rest of the body is, and along the way he will come of age, realize that evil lurks in his hometown, and be confronted by the great white whale of a woman's body. Is that Isabella Rossellini in the front garden, rising up, naked and pale? It's only a movie.

1987: *Fatal Attraction*

Here's a title Hitch might have liked and a story that had his kind of urbane, urban people—though Hitch would have us anticipate from Glenn Close's hair that she might go crazy. When Michael Douglas has a brief fling, the sexual passion gets out of control. (Like any voyeur, Hitch knows that attraction can be fatal—the eyes read too much into it. Desire wants too much, like happiness or paradise.) But the woman's need is so great that, once abandoned, she becomes a killer. There was no need to play this one for laughs, but a lethal irony operated throughout, and in the end Hitchcock would surely have liked the pressure on people to take responsibility for their own actions. You shouldn't fuck with fucking, the film says—though, of course, films everywhere were by then encouraging just that.

1991: *The Silence of the Lambs*

Here was a slasher film turned into an A production by Jonathan Demme, and winning the Oscar for Best Picture—just a little story about a birdlike student at the FBI academy, Clarice Starling, on the track of a grisly serial killer, with an awful uncle figure tucked away in prison who may help her because he likes her smell. It's cannibalism-turned-gourmet, and the film plainly ends with Hannibal Lecter and his Diners Club card on a spree, and good luck to them. What was most indicative of the new standards was how such peeled skin, sensationalism, and sadism could be cooked and served as a Best Picture dish instead of a concession to grim times. By the sequel, Hannibal Lecter was nearly a great lover—the star authority of Anthony Hopkins had rehabilitated the role and the cannibal. So children all over America (they can see an R-rated film if they are "with" a moral guardian) were doing the fava beans and Chianti line and fluttering their tongues.

1995: *Pulp Fiction*

The story keeps shifting, but in the end it will come back with a vengeance, like a snake ready to eat its own tail. Yes, we can believe that Quentin Tarantino had seen every Hitchcock film in the video store before he was grown up. The real question is when is he planning to be grown up, and has the regimen of Hitchcock delayed that great day? Mr. Wolf (Harvey Keitel), that chatty specialist in rapid tidying-up operations, obviously has a lot of Norman Bates in him.

1998: *Psycho*

———————————

This is the remake, in color, but from the same script and often shot for shot. This fatuous duplication is very handy, for Gus Van Sant's per-shot pressure is scarcely measurable, whereas in Hitchcock it is unbearable. (Van Sant was only eight when *Psycho* opened—too young to be allowed to see it.) Anne Heche is Marion, Viggo Mortensen is Sam, Vince Vaughan is Norman, Julianne Moore is Lila, William H. Macy is Arbogast, Philip Baker Hall is the sheriff, and Robert Foster is the psychiatrist. Of course, we can see productions of *Hamlet*, *The Cherry Orchard*, and *The Homecoming* all our lives, pointing out the differences, whereas to see just one remake like this teaches us that the amalgam of casting, atmosphere, and the moment is always unique. Janet Leigh and Anthony Perkins are so missing (not to mention missed) that you begin to realize anew just what an indirect love story Hitchcock had left in 1960: $40,000 has become $400,000, Norman has lost his Eroica Symphony recording (he has a Tammi Wynette and George Jones album instead), and he has a pornographic magazine—as if Mother would have let that in the house.

2009: *Red Riding*

There's something appropriate in this return to England, if only because, prodded along by George Orwell, Agatha Christie, Alfred Hitchcock, and a long line of serial killers, the English have developed a great interest in murder, in part scholarly, in part grisly, in part at the level of speculative gossip about the neighbors. *Red Riding* is a three-movie TV series adapted from four novels by David Peace that are based loosely on the case of the "Yorkshire Ripper," a man named Peter Sutcliffe who killed a series of prostitutes before he was captured and then confined at Broadmoor, the country's prison for the criminally insane.

Like the novels, the TV series is a work of fiction, strongly augmented by local knowledge and rooted in a sense of massive police corruption—politically, indeed, it is an attack on Yorkshire as a kind of private but wild kingdom where the police do as they wish. Directed by three different people, the TV series is not easy to follow. Its mood is grim in the extreme, but it does not really dwell on the killings of women and children, and overall it is a superb attempt to treat psychotic crime in the context of a dysfunctional society. Thus, it tends to spell out something only hinted at in *Psycho:* that troubled societies may breed psychos. Of course, that idea can be read as a sentimental interpretation by dismayed liberals—so far, the rambunctious, guilt-free serial killer is still an oddity. But this is bloodied territory, and there's money in the blood.

7

A Noir Society

IN WAYS OVER WHICH Alfred Hitchcock had little aware-
ness, the world was ready for him in 1960. Television
was a medium that could cut instantaneously and without
sentiment or irony from the lavishly engraved stylization
of commercials to the rawest of documentary footage of an
automobile disaster, the scene of a murder, or the trail of
warfare. In the '60s, television "taste" yielded to increasingly graphic violence from Vietnam, Biafra, and so many
other places and put them in its own dramas. The world became a montage, or a collage, easily perceived as madness
even though a piece of ordinary furniture kept it in place.
There was no way that television could pretend to be in
control, or protecting us. The old Hollywood had been
dead long enough for its code of security and happiness to

be not just ruined but mocked. Disaster was in the air, and coast-to-coast live coverage waited to eat it up. Being a movie star was no protection: ask Janet Leigh.

November 22, 1963, produced a fragment of film that would be more scrutinized than anything since the Odessa steps sequence in *Battleship Potemkin*. A man named Abraham Zapruder had been in Dealey Plaza, Dallas, as the president drove by. His super 8mm camera was photographing the John F. Kennedy motorcade, and in less than four hundred frames he recorded something that would be pored over by experts and scholars for decades. Within the blur of those frames there was a man being killed, over and over again, with pieces of his head blown into the air. But technicalities obscured the tragedy, as the Zapruder film became the time line for what had occurred in Dealey Plaza and the footage itself was the means of a debate over when people were struck by bullets and where the shooter or shooters might have been. The filmstrip allowed a daylight robbery of life and history; it was darkness at noon as noir took over the news.

This was film analysis made available, and urgent, for everyone. It was also a lesson in the nature of television and its openness to so many styles or genre assumptions. The same television screen could show fantasy and unimpeachable actuality without a blink. Young people (learning in the 1960s to doubt America) began to ask questions about the reliability of what they were seeing. The sudden stylistic anthology made available (by a medium that early on turned to old movies to fill its hours) was a terrific stimulus to questions on the nature of film, on criticism and history. In the space of a few years in the early sixties the readership for serious writing on films increased. Kids going to college looked at the curriculum and asked why there were no courses on film.

As censorship relaxed, and as more graphic versions of sex and violence reached the screen, so another new expertise got under way. It was called "special effects," and it meant using the resources of the medium to show things not previously seen. Some of this seemed harmless, and beautiful—like the first dissolves. You could show bodies falling—actors pretending to be shot—in slow motion, and it seemed "balletic." If you then sewed sachets of vegetable dye into the actors' costumes and set tiny charges to explode this "blood," why, then, you could give the impression of bodies broken by bullets, of blood spurting out, of gobbets of flesh breaking away. This is the cinema of Sam Peckinpah (among others), and there was a poet inside him as well as a man drunk on destruction. But some who followed Peckinpah forgot or were incapable of any balancing need for poetry, for compassion for those characters shot to pieces.

In time, the ingenuity of special effects soared ahead—it is the fundamental creative explosion in modern filmmaking, made at the expense of deeper imaginative thought, and it left the human context way behind. The movies had always loved new special effects, and sought them—*Citizen Kane*, for example, is full of them. (Remember, as it began, movie was itself a very special effect; story came later.) But in the years after about 1970, the ability of these effects, culminating in computer-generated images, to release violence was beyond question and out of control. All too often, it was a "fun ride" separated from pain, damage, and consequence.

There is no need to blame Alfred Hitchcock alone for this development—it is rooted in the culture as a whole. But *Psycho* more than any one film had said, "Forget the consequences of a case study if the end product is thrilling enough." Thus, a substantial thing had been posited—Norman Bates as the deranged killer—but only to make another kind of killing.

What was lost in that process was Hitchcock's unique jaundiced vision—the thing stressed in the first forty min-

utes of *Psycho:* his sense of the unkind society. And surely
this charge is just, or at least hard to dismiss: in the end,
Hitch had not cared enough for his own creation, for Norman. In 1965, talking of his own film *Pierrot le Fou* and de-
fending himself against charges that it had too much
blood, Jean-Luc Godard said, "That's not blood—it's just
red." It was a smart-ass remark, showing how limited
young intelligence can be. To rephrase Godard himself, the
aesthetics of cinema rely on a sense of its ethics. But Godard's gloss was not far from Hitchcock's own noncha-
lance when challenged with gruesomeness or tragedy. He
would say, "It's only a movie," and thus the chic coverlet
of "noir" was drawn up to conceal the human pain.

Alfred Hitchcock had yearned to make movie important, respectable, and artlike. He had achieved an interna-
tional sensation and helped establish the power of the
director as auteur. But he had also isolated films from the
larger horizons of meaning.

IN THE GREAT RAGE FOR HITCHCOCK and his droll state-
ments about himself, *Psycho* was a central piece of cool.
You could say the film was exploitation: trash and sex and
violence. But no one seeing it for the first time ever felt
that was a sufficient description. *Psycho* was the new

American film, and the assurance in its maker of having a bit of fun with so much blood seemed like a new attitude for what would soon be regarded as the swinging and insouciant sixties.

The change was sharpened by controversy. The French regard for Hitchcock had washed up on English-speaking shores very slowly. In London the *Cahiers* writers were thought to be too young, often incoherent hero worshipers. The English liked to think they knew their Hitchcock and his amiable fraud. In England an attitude had set in that Hitch was an "entertainer"—not a serious filmmaker. He was excluded from gravity by such things as nuns in high-heeled shoes, the wicked use of national monuments, and that old sneaking habit of dainty murder— dainty in that the violence was offset by the meringue of style. It was like the divide Graham Greene made in his own fiction, between entertainments and novels.

But Andrew Sarris in America was a much happier reader of the French. In the spring 1963 issue of *Film Culture*, Sarris arranged a hierarchy of American directors in which the top group was "Pantheon." It included Hitchcock. The article on Hitchcock (later a part of Sarris's book *The American Cinema*) began, "Alfred Hitchcock is the supreme technician of the American cinema. Even his many enemies cannot begrudge him that distinction. Like [John] Ford, Hitchcock cuts in his mind, and not in the cutting room with different set-ups for every scene. His is the only contemporary style that unites the divergent classical traditions of Murnau (camera movement) and Eisenstein (montage). . . . Unfortunately, Hitchcock seldom receives the visual analysis he deserves in the learned Anglo-American periodicals devoted ostensibly to the art of the cinema."

At almost the same time, in London, Penelope Houston, the editor of *Sight and Sound*, wrote a lengthy essay, "The Figure in the Carpet," which addressed the rising passion for Hitchcock (and French ideas). This was epitomized by the appearance in London, in June 1962, of a lively new magazine, *Movie*, the forum for several writers (like V. F. Perkins) who had met at *Oxford Opinion*. *Movie* had published its own "Pantheon," and there were just two directors in the "great" category—Howard Hawks and Hitchcock (actually it came out "Hitchcocl" because of a deflating misprint).

Penelope Houston's essay began by gathering reviews of *The Birds*: Pauline Kael had called it "a bad picture at every level," Ernest Callenbach regarded it as "disappointing . . . made on two mistaken assumptions," but Andrew

Sarris said it was "Hitchcock at the height of his artistic powers." Houston took off from that with great skill to point out the potential follies in the auteur theory—not a difficult task—and the dangers of taking Hitchcock too seriously. She was astute enough to quote Hitchcock sometimes as a way of bringing airy admiration down with a bump: "One of the *Movie* writers found traces of tragedy in *Psycho*. Hitchcock's own comment when interviewed recently by the magazine: 'It was made with quite a sense of fun on my part . . . It's rather like taking the audience through the haunted house at a fairground. After all, it stands to reason that if one were seriously doing the *Psycho* story it would be a case history.'"

I have tried to argue that *Psycho* is undermined by its own failure to believe in the case history, let alone deliver an explanation for it. But it's clear how much Hitchcock's own case dramatized his increasing significance in academe, where he was being taught by dejected English professors who had found that their students, while lacking the stamina for *Middlemarch* or Proust, might have fun with *Psycho*. And in academe everything is turned into politics: thus, the diminution in English departments that begins around 1960 is accelerated by film or "media" programs, and then by business and computer studies (the two disciplines that have most depleted English and the "humanities").

It's notable that Pauline Kael never picked on Hitchcock as a hero. She was the best writer and the most ambitious ideologue in the new critical movement. Her aggressive writing style could surely have made a feast of Hitchcock, just as Kael personally was not far from Hitch the tease and the barbed conversationalist. But Kael was wary, and in 1966 she wrote, "There are movie directors who try to plan out every detail in advance: Hitchcock, for example, conceives the movie visually from the beginning of the script preparation, designing the production like a complicated mouse-trap, then building it. His script is a set of plans representing the completed film, including the editing, and if he doesn't need to depart from it, that is because he works for exactly calculated effects of suspense and perversity. He is an ingenious, masterly builder of mousetraps, and more often than not, the audience is caught tight; his techniques, however, probably have more to do with gamesmanship than with art, and they are almost the opposite of the working methods of most great directors for whom making the movie is itself a process of discovery." (In the early '70s, those comments were fair. The future of the movies seemed to rest in the hands of more open-minded stylistic explorers: Godard, Antonioni, the school of Renoir, Ophuls, Welles, and others open to the accidental moment. Today, cold-blooded planning— Hitchcockian blueprints—has taken the movies back, with a vengeance.)

In the four or five years after *Psycho*, there was more thinking (and writing) about Hitchcock than in the twenty years before. And some of it was outstanding. It was in 1965 that the English critic (and Leavisite) Robin Wood published a short book, *Hitchcock*, and a great step forward in serious film criticism coming from England. Wood was devoted to Hitchcock, and he broached fascinating territory—of real relevance in film studies—in arguing that sometimes a filmmaker didn't know what his work was all about. For example, here is Wood on *Psycho:* "*Psycho* is one of the key works of our age. Its themes are of course not new—obvious forerunners include *Macbeth* and Conrad's *Heart of Darkness*—but the intensity and horror of their treatment and the fact that they are here grounded in sex belong to the age that has witnessed on the one hand the discoveries of Freudian psychology and on the other the concentration camps. I do not think I am being callous in citing the camps in relation to a work of popular entertainment. . . . But one cannot contemplate the camps without confronting two aspects of their horror: the utter helplessness and innocence of the victims, and the fact that human beings, whose potentialities all of us in some measure share, were their tormentors and butchers."

This doesn't heal the wounds in the second part of the film, but it is superb insight on the first part. And for the moment, I return to the points I made earlier, that this was an America not seen or felt before on-screen and that the humor by which the film's most demented character understands that society is not funny enough to take off the chill. The thing I have called "nastiness"—a noir disillusion with the dream of happiness—was about to overtake not just the American movie but the nation's way of life.

THE SLIPPAGE in Hollywood's power could not be ignored as the '60s advanced: average weekly attendance in American theaters dropped from 30 million in 1960 to 18 million in 1969. In the same years the percentage of American households with television increased from 87 to 95. The first moguls (from Mayer to Selznick, from Zanuck to Zukor) were dead or dying. Eighteen million tickets a week was a parlous number when more than 100 million were watching TV for at least six hours a week. The industry, to the extent that it could be located, was suddenly alarmed by the question of what to do. Still, for the moment at least, this logic was offered: if television is soaking up the viewing energies of the ordinary American, then maybe cinema remains available for dark, tough, difficult pictures, films that portray the real America and not just the fantasy idea, films that are there for new young people, for directors with more ambition than budget, for people who perhaps deserve to be treated as auteurs or artists.

In the late '60s and early '70s, American film experienced a new halcyon age—call it the silver years. This new mood certainly didn't cover everything being made. But it gave big jobs to film buffs, to kids just out of film school, to people who were as expert in the history of film as Truffaut and Godard had been.

The films were often dark. They seldom had happy endings. But they were pictures of an authentic American paranoia, something trained in us by the events of the '60s, but something also instilled by abstract expressionist painting; the novels of Mailer, Bellow, and Styron; the uncovering of dysfunction in the plays of Williams and O'Neill; the lament in the voice of Miles Davis; and the sense of wasteland that I have talked about in *Psycho*, to say nothing of the terrible American failure in Vietnam and the domestic agony over civil rights.

Hitchcock is amazingly unaware of these things. He has no black characters in his films. He hardly believes in any social groups. But you can feel the beating pulse that is afraid of disorder, or the lack of order. It is not too great a step to go from birds ready to attack mankind to a shark fit to swallow the camera and its crew.

Jaws is a key picture in the transitions we are looking at. It starts out as a jaded look at a resort community where the local authorities will downplay shark fears to protect their tourist business. This is the new realism of the '70s, and you can see how *Psycho* helped bring it into being. But then the film shifts. It says giant sharks (as hostile as birds) do exist—look, isn't that a fin over there? Gotcha!

There have been isolated shark attacks off American shores as long as people have gone into the water. It's wise to take care—after all, the ocean claims more lives than the sharks. But there are not giant predators such as might eat a small boat or a ham actor. There are not monsters of which you should "Be Afraid—Be Very Afraid!" That is the language of sensationalist entertainment, cheerfully promoting unreal threats.

8

Lonely People

THERE ARE LONELY PEOPLE with small, hopeless roles in Hitchcock films, and they linger in our memory. They spring from a fear that may be graver than the one that dreads knives in the shower. They are what are called "supporting" parts, yet support is what they lack most. Take the wife in *The Wrong Man* as played by Vera Miles. At first she is the wife and mother who cannot understand why her husband, Manny Balastrero, has been arrested for a few local robberies. She rallies to his side. But as their ordeal is prolonged, the stress is too much for her. Manny's lawyer sees that the wife is having a breakdown. It had seemed like Manny's story, because he is the wrong man (falsely accused). But finally it is a film about a woman, so Manny is wrong again, and helpless with his wife's illness.

There is "Miss Lonelyhearts" in *Rear Window*, whose suicide attempt nearly gets in the way of the adventure. There is Annie (Suzanne Pleshette) in *The Birds*, the victim of Mitch's arrogance, Lydia's need to control, and Annie's own depressive passivity. There is Lila in *Psycho*—whatever is going to happen to her? There is Barbara Bel Geddes in *Vertigo*, always waiting for Scottie, yet hardly noticed. You could say there is Judy in *Vertigo*—the other Novak role—hired in as a stooge but never able to lay hold on her own life.

And there is Lars Thorwald in *Rear Window*. Thorwald hardly speaks in his film, let alone testifies on his own behalf. But we can see how nagged and alienated he is. It's not that he has another woman, it's just that he longs to be free of his wife's tirade. So he kills her and then hopes for peace to settle on him as he smokes a cigarette in the dark. Instead, he is hounded and tormented by Jimmy Stewart's cold gaze. And that suspicion proves correct: Thorwald is the murderer. But when he confronts Stewart with the pathetic question "What do you want of me?" we can see that the murder accusation is hardly an adequate explanation of or solution to Thorwald's unhappy life. He wanted quiet and rest—and it cannot be.

But Thorwald's hope stays with you, and Norman Bates brings it back to life.

In the last analysis, that loneliness is more interesting in *Psycho*, and more pioneering, than the violence, the sex, or the terrific assertion of "pure" cinema. For the first fifty or so years of film's history, the quality that had kept it short of art was the fabulous, positive togetherness of its mood. It was an entertainment for crowds—the largest, least-discriminating crowds the world had ever known. The "we" in the dark laughed, cried, and shuddered in concert. And there was constant reassurance in the medium—that everything will be all right, that "they" lived happily ever after, that humanity is a shared bond and duty. This was something wonderful, as witnessed by the collective response to Chaplin and the clowns, to musical creations like Astaire and Garland, to ninety minutes of silly bliss, to such giddy romances as *Casablanca*, *Gone With the Wind*, and *The Wizard of Oz*, or even *The Best Years of Our Lives*, where the word *Our* means something directly related to the *United* in "the *United* States."

So movies strove to let us think well of ourselves. They wanted to promote the crowd in the dark as a neat model for society. Yet in the first fifty years of the twentieth century (the halcyon years of movie) the older arts moved toward an almost inescapable condition of existential loneliness or isolation in which the artwork was both an expression of and a tribute to private experience.

As I have tried to show, Hitchcock and *Psycho* spearheaded an uncertain but heartfelt urge in some popular filmmakers to be regarded as lonely artists. That is why I stressed the abrasive indifference that *Psycho* uncovers in its first forty minutes — not just the nagging hostility in the small roles, but the fatalism that hangs over Sam and Marion. That is why Norman's attempt to be decent and communicative is unexpectedly humane and valiant.

But the thread of personal alienation runs all the way through the film. For instance, remind yourself to what extent *Psycho* is a rural or pastoral film — something rare in Hitchcock's work. So the latter part of the film is set in the country town of Fairvale; the name is chosen carefully, and its irony has time to sink in. Fairvale is the sort of place that had been steadily idealized in American films, no matter that, at the same time, those towns and areas may have run out of population. It is the world of some Frank Capra films, of many comedies and romances. It is the "home" called Kansas in *The Wizard of Oz*. It is the Santa Rosa,

California, where Hitchcock set *Shadow of a Doubt*, and he imagines a close, if not claustrophobic, community on the edge of gossip and a barely contained hysteria. (He finds the same mood in the town diner in *The Birds*, set in Bodega Bay.)

In *Psycho*, the community is sketched in briefly but expertly in the form of the sheriff and his wife, the grim hardware store and the Sunday morning churchgoing. Casting John McIntire as the sheriff was a way of saying, "Surely you know this place and these people—you can trust them." The sheriff and Norman are on a first-name basis. The sheriff knows he can call Norman on the phone. He trusts what he hears in that talk. Yet the sheriff knows nothing about the private world of Norman Bates, and he has no notion of the kind of life he has been leading for years. (We learn later, in the explanation scene, that two other girls disappeared in recent years—without any satisfactory conclusion.)

The idea of community is hollow. That is why the interior of the Bates house and its tomblike bedrooms feel removed from any other world. What makes Norman so eloquent in that nighttime talk with Marion is the instinct that he may never have another chance to speak naturally to anyone. That's what the film is about: not just that madmen lurk in houses on country roads but that loneliness can drive you mad.

That's why it's so important to feel so little prospect of marriage between Sam and Marion in *Psycho*, as well as the eerie indicator that Marion has just met her most understanding man as she steps into the shower. That's why she looks like an angel in the stream of water from the shower, purified and transcendent. Of course, she's mistaken. She hasn't read the meeting quite right. But that happens a lot in Hitchcock. In *Vertigo*, at Ernie's restaurant Scottie marvels that "Madeleine" stands so close to him so that he drinks in her beauty and her mysterious presence without ever realizing why she is standing so still and so close to him. He can look and see and have the ring in his nose forever afterward.

Hitchcock knew that a system locked into watching and seeing can misread its surroundings and can even lose its identity and ordinary human sympathies because of the pressure of voyeurism. The voyeurism is so heavy, so forceful, it can smother real human nature. *Psycho* is the conclusion to a set of films beginning with *Rear Window*, and for me that is Hitchcock's best film in that the smile of satisfaction at the end covers without hiding the loneliness that affects the people. *Rear Window* is a romance, a comedy, and a thriller, but a portrait of alienation, too. The apartments and the windows are screens, of course, but they are traps, or cells—in that entire courtyard no one seems to "know" anyone else; neighborliness has not been invented.

One way to read *Psycho* is be careful, be afraid, for every time you set out on the road you run the risk not just of finding your destination but of being waylaid by chance, and then of being swept away by it. That's the impulse that began with *Strangers on a Train*, the intuition that the glib, flimsy morality of Guy Haines cannot withstand the intricate insights of the madman, Bruno Anthony. Most of Hitchcock's madmen are rich in understanding; it is a gift that comes with their estrangement. And that's part of the pain in *Vertigo*—that the distraught detective sees only the resemblance between two Kim Novaks, not that they are the same tormenting person.

Hitchcock is vulnerable to charges of being unworldly, of being an odd and archaic Englishman in America. And it's true that the rough, vast America seldom gets into his films. But sometimes it is there—for example, in that moment in *Shadow of a Doubt* when Uncle Charlie crosses a piece of urban wasteland and we realize his madness is in the grain of a shabby nation, and on the highway in *Psycho* as Marion Crane's paranoia spills down on her car with the rain, the rain that promises water and blood. In such moments, Hitchcock transcends his grimly tidy plots and suddenly reveals the sensibility of someone lost in a wasteland, afraid of fear and the desolation.

9

On the Way to Fairvale

IF IT'S JUST YOU DRIVING, you can come clear across the country in five days, averaging six hundred miles a day, like a knife through butter. You should stop for an hour a couple of times a day unless you've done work driving, because you won't know how tired you are getting. And you don't want to wake up just before you collide with an eighteen-wheeler filled with gasoline or toxic chemicals or nuclear waste. So you'll likely want to be on the road by six in the morning, and there'll be time to ask yourself—as the Texas preacher talking in tongues turns into Navajo radio—whether you're going mad or having the time of your life. With the roadkill crunching under your wheels like granola. It'll be okay in the end because you'll come back into urbanization, another version of the best facilities you left on the East Coast. But three or four days of your trip you're going to be driving through distance itself, where there seems to be just the road carrying you along. And then you realize that in America the poetry is often in the official signage, the poker-faced information that you're on the "interstate." Think of that word in terms of *Psycho*, of Marion's face dissolving into Norman's, of little spurts of craziness carrying people away. The interstate is the passion for becoming somewhere else. There are places in America where you can be driving in nothing and then you see the Emerald City (Las Vegas) lined up on the horizon like bowling pins ready to be scattered. You may not understand America, but you can drive it.

I have driven I-5 quite a lot these last few years, going up into northern California, passing between San Francisco and Sacramento, going over the flat, burned fields that are close to desert in summer, and then feeling the land rise at Red Bluff and Redding and getting up to Shasta, where the mountain has snow on its cone year-round, like a wedding cake. And I know a lot of the motels in that area.

You must not be put off by them just because of *Psycho*. It really is safer to stop at the motel instead of pulling your car over on the soft shoulder and trying to sleep there at night. The people who run the motels are friendly. The places are cheap and clean and large. And they are near diners where you can eat well, especially if you settle for breakfast every meal. I recommend it as a way to see the country.

You see, divas like Norman Bates don't actually get to run motels. It's too much work. You have to have the linen changed every day. You need the bathrooms cleaned. You don't do it yourself. Because you're in the office checking the folks in and out, making sure the sachets of coffee and the soap and the shampoo are in every room every night, and making sure the televisions and the phones work. And being ready to tell visitors the best place to go for white water rafting, or to see the caves or the redwoods, or simply to talk, because sometimes if people have driven six hundred miles a day they are just hungry for talk— hungrier for that than for the All-American slam breakfast which gets you three eggs cooked to your choice, with bacon, sausage, or ham, two pancakes, hash brown potatoes with toast (white, wheat, rye, or sourdough), fresh OJ, and keep-the-coffee-coming. If you're having coffee on the road, you get as many cups as you want, darling, and you bet we're going to keep calling it OJ, even if he was a murderer. A little bit of melodrama never put us off.

Oh, sure, there are motels that were bypassed when they brought the interstate in, but those places didn't last as motels more than a few months. And then Norman would have been off, joining the Marines or moving into Fairvale to work in the pet store, or joining the police force. If you really wanted to remake *Psycho*, try the idea of Norman as that dark-glasses superhero, not even breathless, who gets to pull some Marion over and tell her he clocked her at 105 mph.

"Oh, officer, I must have been dreaming."

"Really. Well, ma'am, do I look like a dream or what?"

And the folklore then likes to tell you that the lady in the car pulls at her skirt a little and very soon has Officer Norman in the back, and no questions asked.

Hitchhikers? Well, there are stretches by prisons where you aren't supposed to stop the car, let alone pick up anyone walking. But hitchhiking is less common these days—no matter that the movie nightmare remains very popular, where you pick up this fellow and he's straight from hell. Or he's Howard Hughes, and he'll remember you in his will, for just half an hour of talk. They all want to talk.

I wouldn't worry about the motels or the hitchhikers, not nearly as much as the fact that at 65 mph any little disorder on the highway can quickly turn into a slow section, where the traffic coming the other way drops down to a crawl to see how the medics are slipping the bloody bodies out of the torn steel. The highway can be a war zone in seconds, and the traffic casualties we suffer on the interstates have all the wars beaten flat.

Not that I'd blame the freeway system. If you've got a country three thousand miles by fifteen hundred, more or less, you've got to have a way of getting there. After all, it was a brave thing for Nevada to say "Let's have quickie divorces and gambling" in 1931. But it's hardly worth doing without Interstate 80 getting you from San Francisco to Reno or I-15 from L.A. to Vegas. And what made Bugsy Siegel see the point of Las Vegas (which barely existed in 1940) was that the highway to Los Angeles could get people there for a weekend. Sure, that highway is a bit of a gamble, too, because everyone goes too fast and tailgates on that road. Nevada was never founded on the idea of taming recklessness.

So don't be put off by the driving or the highways. Don't ever think as you come across I-50 in Nevada, which just like a character in a noir movie advertises itself as "the loneliest highway in the world," don't ever say to yourself, "What if I broke down here?"

As a matter of fact, the freeways are things America does very well. It's as if some team of frontier scouts and landscape architects shaped them to the country. Sure, there are hundred-mile straightaways—there have to be—but so much of the time the roads are a joy to drive and the unfolding views are done with skill and taste. If only the country could do education, welfare, health with the same grace. So many American cities are drab—like Phoenix. But nearly any stretch of the interstate is beautiful and uniquely American. It's like a great track, and you won't understand the appeal of NASCAR in America without seeing that it's a vision of driving before there was law.

I know there were hitchhikers once, like Vag in Dos Passos's *U.S.A.*, or like Montgomery Clift at the start of *A Place in the Sun*, where he's out on the highway thumbing and the great poster of a girl in a white bathing suit stands for journey and destination. "A Place in the Sun" was the motto inscribed on the exterior wall of the Sands hotel/casino which opened in Las Vegas the year after that movie came out. And, theoretically, A Place in the Sun was the assertion that by entering the hotel/casino you were going to win. Of course, that is one of the lies, for anyone who is into the numbers in Vegas will tell you that the majority of us have to lose and go away and be the Norman Bates of the world, caring but saying we don't care.

Do you recollect that moment in *Psycho*? Marion has heard the voice of Mother—it has its own PA system, a weak old woman crystal clear at fifty yards! And Norman admits to Marion that Mother's voice is his "trap." "I was born in mine," he says. "I don't mind it anymore." And she tells him, "Oh, you should. You should mind it." And that's when Norman, or Perkins, gives one of his tiny shrugs—heartbreaking yet lyrically self-denying: "Oh, I do—but I say I don't." An alarm bell could go off there, saying "possible psychotic reaction." Yet the more I think about this Norman-and-Mother thing, the more I see Norman as one of those lifelong actors who just does Mother and can't get her out of his head now. It's not that Norman Bates is fleeing from some terrible wrath—he's looking for belief, for someone to be. He's just one more of those dark, solitary people living alone, the kind that Hitchcock can hardly stop himself from showing us. The kind like him, the kind that would never resort to the violence played with in movies but who cannot give up the dream.

THERE'S A DETAIL in Donald Spoto's biography of Hitchcock that I can never forget. Alfred had a wardrobe with six or a dozen versions of the same dark suit, with plain shirts and ties and shoes to go with it. He wore just that one costume. And he had only ever made love to his wife, Alma, and that not for years. Of course, this fellow was famous and he lived in Beverly Hills, so the fixed limits of his life were easily overlooked. Think of him in some kind of Fairvale with all the same suits, turning the lights on and off, doing his voices, running stories in his head in which sometimes the lonely people blunder into blind-chance meeting and all of us see motels as unlucky mortuaries.

Looking at the last days of Alfred Hitchcock is not cheerful. One book says he had a pretty secretary and they just sat on opposite sides of the room watching each other masturbate. Now take another look at the supper scene in the office. Gotcha. The loneliness he had ignored or fought away came home to roost. And it was harder for him or anyone to deny that community in the world had given way to a vision of murder as the new orthodoxy. Yet it is wrong with Hitch to be so gloomy as to yield to all of that. His abiding character as an artist—and that survives the man—has to do with the humor he kept in reserve. So *Psycho* is not just a hundred screams and strikes of the knife, it's also, "My mother isn't quite herself today." It's poker-faced irony.

Here is that Hitch at his best, very English, suave and detached, teasing yet truthful, at the 1974 honors given him by the Film Society of Lincoln Center: "As you have seen, murder seems to be the prominent theme. As I do not approve of the current wave of violence that we see on our screens, I have always felt that murder should be treated delicately. And, in addition to that, with the help of television, murder should be brought into the home where it rightly belongs. Some of our most exquisite murders have been domestic: performed with tenderness in simple, homey places like the kitchen table or the bathtub. Nothing is more revolting to my sense of decency than the underworld thug who is able to murder anyone—even people to whom he has not been properly introduced. After all, I'm sure you will agree that murder can be so much more charming and enjoyable, even for the victim, if the surroundings are pleasant and the people involved are ladies and gentlemen like yourselves."

So don't be too afraid of the motels and the road but watch out for the ladies and gentlemen.

ACKNOWLEDGMENTS

Of course, I want to thank those who made this book possible—Lara Heimert, its editor; Sandra Beris, the project editor; and Steve Wasserman, the agent who helped set it up. I also feel I have been talking to some people about *Psycho* for fifty years and I thank—among others—Kieran Hickey, Patrick McGilligan, Janet Leigh, and my wife, Lucy Gray, author of a fascinating play about Hitchcock and his wife, Alma.

But I want to thank the film, too, for the way from the start it was so clearly both a fevered hot work (terrifying) and a very cool demonstration of the thing called movie (comic). Being so Nabokovian, it was one of the films that set me writing, and I still love to see it and its fellows, including Douglas Gordon's immense, slowed-down version which takes about twenty-four hours to see—not that I have yet had all that time.

CREDITS

1960

Psycho, 1960, a Shamley production, a Paramount release. Directed by Alfred Hitchcock; screenplay, Joseph Stefano, from the novel by Robert Bloch; director of photography, John L. Russell; art direction, Joseph Hurley and Robert Clatworthy; set decoration, George Milo; unit manager, Lew Leary; titles, Saul Bass; editor, George Tomasini; costume supervisor, Helen Colvig; makeup supervision, Jack Barron and Robert Dawn; hairstylist, Florence Bush; special effects, Clarence Champagne; sound recording, Waldon O. Watson and William Russell; assistant director, Hilton A. Green; pictorial consultant, Saul Bass; music by Bernard Herrmann.

With Anthony Perkins, Vera Miles, John Gavin, Martin Balsam, John McIntire, Simon Oakland, Vaughn Taylor, Frank Albertson, Lurene Tuttle, Pat Hitchcock, John Anderson, Mort Mills, Paul Jasmin (uncredited), and Janet Leigh as Marion Crane.

Reading

Anobile, Richard J., ed. *Alfred Hitchcock's "Psycho."* London: Picador, 1974. The script is illustrated by frame enlargements.

Auiler, Dan. *"Vertigo": The Making of a Hitchcock Classic.* New York: St. Martin's, 1998.

Bloch, Robert. *Psycho.* New York: Simon and Schuster, 1959.

Chabrol, Claude, and Eric Rohmer. *Hitchcock.* Paris: Éditions Universitaires, 1957.

Conrad, Peter. *The Hitchcock Murders.* London: Faber and Faber, 2000.

Durgnat, Raymond. *A Long Hard Look at "Psycho."* London: British Film Institute, 2002.

Gottlieb, Sidney, ed. *Hitchcock on Hitchcock: Selected Writings and Interviews.* Berkeley and Los Angeles: University of California Press, 1995.

McGilligan, Patrick. *Alfred Hitchcock: A Life in Darkness and Light.* New York: Regan Books, 2003.

Paini, Dominique, and Guy Cogeval. *Hitchcock and Art: Fatales Coincidences.* Montreal: Montreal Museum of Fine Arts, 2001. This is a catalog to a superb exhibition, mounted first in Montreal and then transferred to the Pompidou in Paris—perhaps the greatest art gallery tribute to a filmmaker ever offered.

Rebello, Stephen. *Alfred Hitchcock and the Making of "Psycho."* New York: Dembner, 1990.

Rothman, William. *Hitchcock: The Murderous Gaze.* Cambridge: Harvard University Press, 1982.

Sharff, Stefan. *The Art of Looking at Hitchcock's "Rear Window."* New York: Limelight, 1967.

Skerry, Philip J. *Psycho in the Shower: The History of Cinema's Most Famous Scene.* New York: Continuum, 2009.

Spoto, Donald. *The Dark Side of Genius: The Life of Alfred Hitchcock.* New York: Little, Brown, 1983.

Truffaut, François. *Hitchcock.* New York: Simon and Schuster, 1967.

Wood, Robin. *Hitchcock's Films.* London: Zwemmer, 1965.

_____. *Hitchcock's Films Revisited.* New York: Columbia University Press, 1989.

Zizek, Slavoy, ed. *Everything You Always Wanted to Know About Lacan (but Were Afraid to Ask Hitchcock).* London: Verso, 1992.

INDEX